THE GREYSTON BAKERY COOKBOOK

THE GREYSTON BAKERY COOKBOOK

by Helen Glassman and Susan Postal

Photographs by Lou Manna
Illustrations by Lynn Wohlers

Shambhala
Boston & London
1986

SHAMBHALA PUBLICATIONS, INC.
314 Dartmouth Street
Boston, Massachusetts   02116

9   8   7   6   5   4   3   2   1
First Edition

Printed in the United States of America
Distributed in the United States by Random House
and in Canada by Random House of Canada Ltd.

Library of Congress Cataloging-in-Publication Data
Glassman, Helen.
  The Greyston Bakery cookbook.

  Includes index.
  1. Baking.   I. Postal, Susan.   II. Greyston Bakery.
III. Title.   IV. Title: Cookbook.
TX763.G554   1986   641.7'1   86-11845
ISBN 0-87773-323-6

Typography by Anthea Lingeman

CONTENTS

5. All in a Crust: Tarts and Pies   *91*

6. Happy Endings: Irresistible Cakes   *105*

ACKNOWLEDGMENTS

A month-long scouting and training visit to the Tassajara Bakery convinced us all that we wanted to bake wonderful breads and cakes just as they do. The staff at the Tassajara Bakery took us into their minds and hearts and gave us every little bit of information that they had about ingredients, recipes, mixing, baking, and selling. We owe our basic training and many of our recipes to them. In addition, the People's Bakery in Minneapolis shared their recipes and many of their techniques with us. We were amazed at the generosity of many bakers. Todd of Shana's Bakery in the Bronx and Joe Tarricone of Caffé Puglie in Yonkers were always willing to have us come watch a production technique or discuss a problem on the phone.

The scrumptious and beautiful cakes, breads, and pastries that appear on these pages are due in the final analysis to the bakers who devoted themselves to learning how to make puff pastry and chocolate perform. Formerly a professor, a graphic artist, a mushroom grower, a pianist, a legal secretary, a film editor, a ballerina, and a nursery school teacher, they constantly bought books, called our baker friends, and experimented. To Kosho Ishikawa, Charles Kutler, Ken Sailor, Lou Nordstrom, Henry Mende, Ross Blum, Bryan Rich, Wendy Megerman, Carmelo Pagan, Earl White, Daichi Kuniyasu, and Traci Elyas, many, many thanks.

We want especially to express our appreciation to Mildred Marmur, who first suggested that we write this book.

These delicious desserts are here because friends and food devotees have put in hours of work testing and baking to ensure a delectable result in your kitchen. This book also takes its beautiful and workable shape because our editors know and care about good baking. Many thanks to Emily Hilburn Sell and Kendra Crossen for meticulous attention to the details that will make using this book fun, exciting, and really easy. Finally, a special thanks to our teacher, Tetsugen Glassman Sensei, for his unfailing encouragement in the face of what seemed at times insurmountable odds.

Special thanks for testing and retesting to Nancy Baker, Eileen Brady, Sean Breheney, Barbara Calnan, Mary Campbell, Ann Marie Czyzewski, Claudia Didul, Sally Drummond, Katie Feucht, Wendy Foulke, Mary Funk, Paula Fuld, Sally Hess, Hans and Barbara Hokanson, Anne Kraus, Nancy Mezey, Astrid O'Brien, Susan Pliner, Ellen Risberg, Judy Sherman, Helene Sides, Sue Thomas, Helen Tworkov, Susan Walker, and Debbie Wood.

THE GREYSTON BAKERY COOKBOOK

INTRODUCTION

In 1979 a group of Zen monks, under the direction of Bernard Tetsugen Glassman Sensei, started the Zen Community of New York in Riverdale. The residential and practice center for this ecumenical community was Greyston Seminary, beautifully situated along the Hudson just north of Manhattan. Three years later, in order to become economically self-sufficient and also to provide a setting for work-practice, Greyston Bakery was founded as the community's livelihood. Greyston Bakery is dedicated to preparing special recipes not only to wholesome standards but also to gourmet perfection. We wanted to continue the Zen tradition of mindfulness, hard work, and service, and we hope that our customers taste the spirit and care that we put into each of our fine baked goods. In keeping with our high standards, we use only the freshest and finest natural ingredients available. We bake from scratch, using no commercial mixes or additives of any kind.

This *Greyston Bakery Cookbook* is a presentation of those very same special recipes for the home kitchen. After much experimentation, observation, and discussion with our production crew, we are ready to share with you our baking knowledge, methods, and most important, our wonderful recipes for your enjoyment. In today's world of "Open the box and add water" baking, we think you will find, as we do, that there is satisfaction in cracking eggs, creaming butter, and kneading dough. Although this book is based on the techniques used in our commercial bakery, all the recipes have been tested (and retested) with ingredients and equipment readily available in local stores.

At the Bakery

Greyston Bakery is dedicated to excellence in the art of baking. From the beginning we have been determined to use only the finest and freshest ingredients for all our products. We are concerned with quality in all aspects of our business—not only in the finished product but also in management, sales, and customer relations. Clearly we are not alone in our concern with quality; there seems to be a surge of interest in things made in the old-fashioned, natural way. Perhaps as a reaction to the "instant breakfast," "pop-tart" commercialism that constantly bombards us, there is a growing enthusiasm and appreciation for genuine well-made baked goods.

Initial inspiration and training (as well as many wonderful recipes) came from the Tassajara Bakery of the San Francisco Zen Center. Our monks soon found themselves literally up to their elbows in doughs, batters, and flours for long days and weeks of hands-on training alongside the monks and lay students of Tassajara. After their return, the aroma of poppy seed cake and shortbread cookies emanated from the Greyston Seminary kitchen, where test-baking of recipes was going on. We tested and tasted, and it seemed as if we could put on five pounds just from inhaling the delicious smells. During this period a study of basic equipment was made and purchasing decisions were based on careful research. Among the major equipment acquired was a computer, allowing the gathering and storing of information for sales and accounting as well as for checking recipe costs and scaling charts. In no time computer programs were developed that translated customer orders for the day into pounds of butter and flour for the production crew. Our computer experts have allowed us to expand gracefully and competently in all areas of the business.

After about a year, we outgrew our original bakery site just north of Riverdale in Yonkers and arranged to purchase a larger bakery on the Hudson River in Yonkers on Woodworth Avenue. This site allows us to have two large ovens plus a walk-in refrigerator and a walk-in freezer. An added benefit is that there is ample office space upstairs for sales, accounting, Zen Community offices, and a meditation hall.

One of the crucial questions at the beginning was whether to place the emphasis on wholesale or retail sales. It was decided to move in both directions—to capitalize on the wonderful potential of Manhattan for wholesale sales to restaurants, gourmet shops, and department stores, as well as open up our own retail shop in Riverdale to provide an outlet for our products in the neighborhood of Greyston Seminary. The Greyston Bakery Café was opened on Mosholu Avenue in a building then owned by the community. It has provided a wonderful point of connection between Riverdale residents and the Zen Community. Not only are our neighbors able to buy our delicious products, but we have also offered free Sunday-night musicals and poetry readings. A gallery for photography has made good use of wall space in the café and further emphasized its role as a small cultural arts center for the neighborhood.

In the preholiday flurry of shopping and buying in November 1982 we began to find customers. Our first customer was Neiman-Marcus, and by January 1983 we had forty-five accounts in Manhattan and Westchester. Our opening product line consisted of cakes and cookies. Muffins and scones were introduced one month later, followed by brownies, goldies, and walnut coffee cake. Breads, rolls, and tarts as well as elegant chiffon cakes have now been added to give us a complete bakery line. At present we have a list of about one hundred customers, and over the years we have sold to large organizations like Macy's, the Guggenheim Museum, World Yacht Enterprises, Seaport Line, the Museum of Modern Art, the Russian Tea Room, B. Altman & Co., Balducci's, Dean and DeLuca, and Godiva Chocolatier, and small ones like Butler Brothers in Harrison Bedford Gourmet, and Santangelo's in SoHo. We are in telephone contact with our customers, making every effort to bring them freshly baked goods on a schedule that works well for their businesses. Quality control is important to us, and we regard the occasional customer complaint as a "golden opportunity" to learn how to do a better job.

Many people who work at the bakery are Zen students for whom Greyston Bakery provides the opportunity for work-practice. They come from a great variety of backgrounds, live together at Greyston Seminary or in nearby apartments, study with Glassman Sensei, and spend long hours and tremendous energy working together in the areas of production (divided into cake, bread, and finishing crews), delivery, sales, accounting, computer processing, and administration. Non-community-members who work for the bakery have taught us well and contributed generously from their expertise, allowing us to meet the demands of our growing business without sacrificing our dedication to excellence.

Into Your Kitchen

To write this *Greyston Bakery Cookbook* we have had to move from the production floor to a suburban kitchen and embark on what might be called a "translation" project. Our computer recipes are for large batches—like sixty pans of brownies or twenty cakes—and they use weight measurements such as pounds of flour, not cups, and ounces of baking powder, not teaspoons. First, everything had to be weighed or measured to discover how many cups in a pound of flour, sugar, rolled oats, coconut, walnuts, and so on. Then, armed with a stack of computer print-outs of our whole product line and a handy calculator, we spread everything out on the kitchen table in the effort to reduce the recipes to manageable size. Getting the mathematically correct formula was the easy part.

Fortunately, baking experience made it immediately apparent that there would have to be considerable adjustment of proportions before we would come close to duplicating our products. Just for fun, and to prove this point, the computer was asked to print out the recipe for one Casablanca Cake. The cake was baked exactly as the computer designated and, as expected, was really awful—a dry, small, tasteless ring, which did give us lots of laughs. From then on it was a question of adjusting, baking, tasting, over and over. There were days of disasters, when batches of muffins went to the birds (and a visiting raccoon who loved the ones with blueberries). The end of the day would often yield a flour-covered kitchen with counters cluttered by cooling cookies and no dinner in sight. No recipe has taken fewer than three tries; some took considerably more. After the recipe was approved, it was farmed out to community members to test in their own kitchens and with their own families. We agreed that the finished pastries had to be essentially identical in taste and appearance to those sold by Greyston Bakery and that there were to be no changes in ingredients except where an ingredient available to the commercial bakery could not be found in local stores.

There seems to be a revival of interest in home baking. We hope that you will come to know the pleasure and satisfaction of using these recipes to make delicious homemade specialties with fresh natural ingredients. We would welcome your experiences, comments, and suggestions in regard to our recipes. Write to us in care of Shambhala Publications, 314 Dartmouth Street, Boston, MA 02116.

1

Great Beginnings

BREAKFAST AND BRUNCH SPECIALTIES

There is something wonderfully old-fashioned about these breakfast breads sweetened with honey or molasses, mixed with fresh eggs, butter, and whole grain flours, and filled with fruits or nuts. These recipes are particularly suited for brunch, when you can serve a tantalizing display of the most delicious things you can garner from your repertoire. Some of these breakfast selections are in the quick-bread (rather than yeast-raised) category, and true to their name they work up quickly and are best served still warm from the oven. However, they can be baked in advance and are fresh for six to twelve hours. All do well when reheated. We also have included a wonderful selection of all-butter Danish pastries that are perfect brunch treats. You may want to prepare several kinds of Danish in advance and freeze them so that on the day of your brunch you need only thaw, proof, and bake.

We have included our original muffin line: Whole Wheat Bran, Cranberry-Orange, and Blueberry. We also offer some muffin varieties still in the research-and-development files: Corn and Maple Nut. Buttermilk Scones, closer to a biscuit than a muffin, are delicious toasted and buttered for breakfast or tea. The Walnut Coffee Cake is an American classic, sprinkled with lots of cinnamon, nuts, and brown sugar. The muffins can be out of the oven and ready to eat about a half-hour after you start mixing. While they are baking there is just time to set the table and scramble the eggs. All these breakfast specialties freeze well if carefully wrapped airtight.

In the yeast-raised department, you will find seven different kinds of butter Danish, each with its own filling and shaping. You will need to allow two to three hours to prepare the basic Danish dough and another two hours for filling, shaping, and proofing—a good project when you are socked in on a rainy day! We also offer fragrant, spiced Hot Cross Buns, a traditional Lenten speciality perfect for Sunday-morning brunches. Finally, and not for Saint Patrick's Day only, this chapter brings you a wonderfully easy Irish Soda Bread.

Whole Wheat Bran Muffins

These muffins have been a favorite of our health food store customers because they combine the whole grain goodness of stoneground wheat with high-fiber bran and are sweetened with honey and molasses. Many of us like to have these Whole Wheat Bran Muffins ready in the freezer (cut in half before tightly wrapping) to pop in the toaster oven for a filling and wholesome breakfast on a busy morning. Studded with plump raisins, they are delicious served warm with butter or cream cheese.

Yield: 10–12 large muffins

¼ cup butter
3 tablespoons honey
3 tablespoons molasses
2 eggs
1 teaspoon pure orange extract
1½ cups whole wheat flour
1 cup whole bran (miller's bran flakes)
½ teaspoon salt
2 teaspoons baking soda
1½ cups buttermilk
½ cup raisins

Preheat oven to 400° F.

Cream butter, honey, and molasses with mixer or by hand.

Add eggs and orange extract, and beat well.

Combine dry ingredients (flour, bran, salt, soda) in separate bowl.

By hand, gradually add dry ingredients, alternating with buttermilk, to the butter mixture. Stir only until everything is evenly moistened.

Fold in raisins.

Spoon into well-buttered muffin tins.

Bake at 400° for 20–25 minutes.

Cool on rack for 5–10 minutes.

Corn Muffins

These are grainy, chewy, not-too-sweet golden muffins made with stoneground whole corn meal, available in health food stores. You could substitute whole wheat pastry flour for the unbleached white for an all-whole-grain muffin that is quite delicious, but not as light.

Yield: 8–10 large muffins

¼ cup butter
3 tablespoons light brown sugar
1 egg, lightly beaten
1 cup whole grain corn meal
1 cup unbleached flour
1 tablespoon baking powder
¾ teaspoon salt
1 cup milk

Preheat oven to 400° F.

Cream butter and sugar, using mixer or wooden spoon.

Add the egg, beating until light.

Separately mix dry ingredients together (corn meal, flour, baking powder, salt).

By hand, gradually stir dry ingredients into butter mixture, alternating with the milk. Mix only until evenly wet; do not beat.

Spoon batter into well-buttered muffin cups almost to the top.

Bake at 400° for 20 minutes.

Turn onto cooling rack for 5 minutes before eating.

Fruit Muffins

In our bakery production we use one muffin base for both the Blueberry Muffins and the Cranberry-Orange Muffins. This base includes whole wheat pastry flour and unbleached white flour, and incorporates mashed ripe banana for moistness and extra sweetness with less sugar. For home baking, the banana is listed as an optional ingredient. If we directly converted our production proportions, it would come out to about one-fourth banana per batch, which seems somehow silly. Adding half a banana gives a definite flavor and makes the texture denser, but it is a very good banana-berry muffin. It's your choice. As with all muffins, it is essential that the batter not be overmixed. Ingredients should be blended just enough to moisten evenly; it is probably best to do this by hand with a big wooden spoon. Fresh berries in season are superb, and they don't "bleed" as much as the frozen ones. You can freeze a bag of fresh cranberries just as they come from the market for later use, if you like.

Yield: about 10 large muffins

1 cup milk
⅓ cup lightly salted butter, melted
1 egg
½ very ripe banana (optional)
1 cup whole wheat pastry flour
1¼ cups unbleached white flour
⅓ cup light brown sugar
⅓ cup granulated sugar
1 tablespoon baking powder
½ teaspoon salt

BLUEBERRY
MUFFINS

1 cup fresh or frozen (without syrup) blueberries, reserving
about 2 tablespoons to sprinkle on the top
1 teaspoon vanilla extract

CRANBERRY-
ORANGE
MUFFINS

1 cup fresh or frozen cranberries, reserving 2 tablespoons for
the top
2 teaspoons dried grated orange rind
2 teaspoons orange extract

Preheat oven to 400° F.

Combine milk, butter, egg, extract, and optional banana, and beat until smooth; an electric mixer is fine.

Separately mix together dry ingredients (flour, sugars, baking powder, salt).

By hand, gradually add liquid mixture to dry ingredients until moistened evenly.

Fold in berries (and orange rind if used), reserving some berries for the top.

Spoon into well-buttered muffin tins almost to the top.

Sprinkle three or four reserved berries on top of each muffin.

Bake at 400° for about 20–25 minutes.

Remove from tins and cool on a rack.

Maple Nut Muffins

This muffin is a variation of our basic recipe. It is a sweeter muffin, with a topping similar to that on our Walnut Coffee Cake.

Yield: 8–10 large muffins

¼ cup lightly salted butter at room temperature
6 tablespoons light brown sugar
1 egg
1 teaspoon maple extract
⅓ cup pure maple syrup
1 cup unbleached flour
1 cup whole wheat pastry flour
1 tablespoon baking powder
½ teaspoon salt
¾ cup milk
¾ cup chopped walnuts or pecans

TOPPING

3 tablespoons brown sugar
3 tablespoons chopped walnuts
1 tablespoon flour

Preheat oven to 400° F.
Cream butter and brown sugar; an electric mixer is fine.
Add egg, extract, and syrup, and beat well.
Separately mix dry ingredients (flours, baking powder, salt).
By hand, gradually add the dry ingredients to the butter mixture alternately with the milk. Stir until evenly moistened.
Fold in nuts, reserving 3 tablespoons for topping.
Spoon into well-buttered muffin tins almost to the top.
Mix together topping in small bowl and sprinkle on muffins.
Bake at 400° for 20 minutes.
Remove from tins and cool on a rack.

Buttermilk Scones

A favorite from the British Isles, these scones are delicious when split and buttered and should always be eaten the day they are made, preferably warm from the oven or toasted.

Yield: 10–12 scones

1 cup unbleached flour
2 cups whole wheat pastry flour
½ teaspoon salt
2½ teaspoons baking powder
½ cup lightly salted butter at room temperature
½ teaspoon orange extract
1 egg
1¼ cups buttermilk
1 cup currants
egg wash: 1 egg beaten with 1 tablespoon water

Preheat oven to 400° F.

Mix the dry ingredients in a large bowl (flours, salt, baking powder).

Cut in the soft butter, using a fork or your fingers, until crumbly and well incorporated.

Beat together the extract, egg, and buttermilk in a small bowl or blender.

Stir the wet mixture into the dry by hand, until evenly moistened.

Add the currants, folding through.

Scoop out onto a well-buttered baking sheet using an ice-cream scoop, forming a rounded mound about 3 inches wide.

Brush with egg wash to glaze.

Bake at 400° for about 20–25 minutes.

Serve warm.

Walnut Coffee Cake

This simple, traditional coffee cake recipe comes from the Tassajara Bakery. The basic two-egg cake batter offers many possibilities for creative touches. One delicious variation included here involves doubling the recipe and baking in a 10-inch bundt pan with the topping swirled in the middle. Use this variation for larger groups of guests or when you want a cake to slice for afternoon coffee. We encourage you to experiment with the topping or filling. How about cocoa and walnuts, apples and cinnamon, or pineapple and brown sugar on the bottom?

Yield: 1 9-inch cake

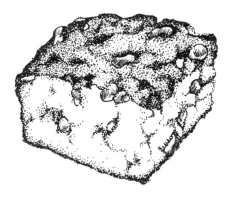

TOPPING

½ cup packed light brown sugar
1 tablespoon flour
1 teaspoon cinnamon
2 tablespoons soft butter
½ cup chopped walnuts (or more to taste)

CAKE

½ cup softened butter
1 cup packed light brown sugar
2 eggs, lightly beaten
1½ cups unbleached flour
2 teaspoons baking powder
½ teaspoon salt
½ cup milk

Preheat oven to 350° F.
Prepare topping first, mixing ingredients in a small bowl in

the order given with a fork (or your fingers) until you have a crumbly mixture. Set aside.

Cream butter and brown sugar until smooth; an electric mixer is fine here.

Add eggs and beat well until light.

Sift together flour, baking powder, and salt.

Add sifted ingredients alternately with milk, using low speed or mixing by hand. Mix well.

Pour into well-buttered 9-inch square cake pan.

Sprinkle topping mixture over the top evenly.

Bake at 350° for about 35 minutes, checking after 30 minutes. Cake should test done with a toothpick in the center and should be starting to pull away from the sides of the pan.

Cool in the pan on a rack for about 30 minutes for easiest cutting. Keep in pan until served.

Cut into 9 squares or as desired.

Cinnamon Swirl Bundt Cake

With the topping in the middle, this cake makes a large, beautiful ring for a tea or brunch.

Yield: 1 10-inch cake

1 topping recipe (page 14)
coffee cake batter recipe (page 14), doubled
¼ cup powdered sugar

Preheat oven to 350° F.

Make a double batch of the coffee cake batter.

Pour half of it into a well-buttered and floured 10-inch bundt pan.

Sprinkle with all the topping mixture, distributing evenly.

Pour in remaining batter, smoothing the top.

Bake at 350° for about 50 minutes, checking for doneness. Cake should spring back when lightly pressed with fingertip.

Cool for 10 minutes, then loosen and turn onto a rack.

Dust lightly with powdered sugar sifted through a sieve.

BUTTER DANISH

This yeast-raised butter-layered pastry is not often made by the home baker, probably because the process is too time-consuming. You will find it a pleasure to make, however, and very satisfying to form into a variety of shapes with contrasting fillings. Ideally one should make the dough on one day, shape and bake it the next. The completed unbaked Danish can be frozen and then thawed and "proofed" (allowed to rise) at some future time. Because this is a yeast-raised dough, adequate proofing is essential for a tender pastry. Because it is also a butter-layered dough, careful rolling and turning are necessary for a flaky result. The filling recipes are designed so that you can make two kinds of Danish from one batch of dough.

BASIC DANISH
DOUGH

1½ cups sweet butter
1 package dry yeast
½ cup very warm water
2 whole eggs
2 egg yolks
1 cup milk
2 tablespoons soy oil
1 teaspoon orange extract
grated rind of one orange
4 cups unbleached flour plus 1 cup as needed
dash salt
⅓ cup sugar
4 tablespoons flour
egg wash: 1 egg beaten with 2 tablespoons water

APRICOT GLAZE

3 tablespoons apricot preserves
½ cup water
½ cup sugar

Remove butter from refrigerator and let it warm to about 60°—not too soft, but not ice-cold either.

In a large mixing bowl, dissolve yeast in very warm water and stir.

In a small bowl beat together eggs, egg yolks, milk, oil, extract, and orange rind.

In another bowl mix flour, salt, and sugar.

Alternately add the liquid and dry ingredients to the dissolved yeast, stirring to incorporate with each addition.

Form a soft dough, adding extra flour until dough forms a ball and leaves the sides of the bowl.

Place ball in an oiled bowl, turn over, and cover with plastic wrap. Chill in refrigerator while you prepare the butter.

Place cool butter on lightly floured board and knead in 4 tablespoons flour.

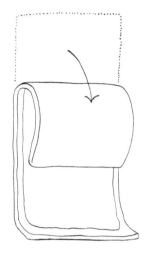

Cover board completely with waxed paper or plastic wrap, tucking in the sides.

Roll out butter on waxed paper with a floured rolling pin, beating it flat as you go. It will be approximately 8 x 16 inches. Lift it off the board with the paper and set the whole sheet flat in the refrigerator to chill while you roll out the dough.

Roll chilled dough on a lightly floured board until it is about ⅛ inch thick and measures about 10 x 20 inches.

Place butter on top of dough by flipping over the waxed paper.

Distribute butter, stretching it and spacing it evenly on top of dough, leaving the outer ½ inch all around butter-free. It is OK if there are small gaps in the butter coverage.

Fold dough into thirds from the top down and from the bottom up, pressing edges together with your hands to seal dough around butter.

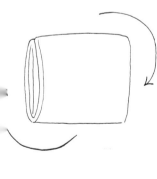

Turn dough vertically (this is your first "turn"), and roll it again to its previous size (about 10 x 20 inches). Fold in thirds as before, wrap in plastic, and chill for a half-hour. (Professionals mark each turn with an indentation made by the index finger in the bottom right corner, so as to keep track of how many turns have been made.)

Repeat this step for two more turns.

After three turns, place the dough in a plastic bag, tie shut, and leave in the refrigerator overnight or for at least 3–4 hours. It will rise in the bag but can be easily pressed down in the morning.

Pick your fillings, and follow the directions for shaping given with each variety. All of the variations that follow are for a regular breakfast-size Danish. You can make delightful mini-Danish by cutting all sizes in half and then reducing the baking time to about 15 minutes. Specific directions for mini-Danish are given at the end of each Danish variation. You still need the full recipe for dough, fillings, egg wash, and glaze, but it all will yield approximately twice as many mini-Danish. You will need to allow 1½ hours to proof both the regular and miniature Danish after they are all formed and filled, before they can go in the oven.

Preheat oven to 350° F.

Brush proofed Danish with egg wash. (Brushing on the egg too early inhibits the rising.)

Bake at 350° for 20–25 minutes, until golden brown.

For a glistening professional finish, lightly brush the hot Danish with a hot Apricot Glaze made by boiling together apricot preserves, water, and sugar. (Note: A simple syrup without preserves will suffice in a pinch.)

Cheese Danish

These cream cheese pockets are a perennial favorite and one of the easiest Danish to shape.

Yield: 12 Danish

½ recipe Basic Danish Dough (page 16), well chilled

CREAM CHEESE
FILLING

1 cup cream cheese at room temperature
1 egg, lightly beaten
3 tablespoons sugar
2 teaspoons vanilla extract
½ teaspoon lemon extract
¼ teaspoon ground cardamom

egg wash
Apricot Glaze

Cream the cream cheese with a wooden spoon until it is very soft and smooth. Add all other filling ingredients in the order given, and mix well.

Divide the batch of Danish dough in half. Reserve the remainder in the refrigerator, well wrapped, awaiting another filling.

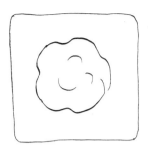

Divide dough in half again, keeping one of the halves wrapped and refrigerated.

Roll out on a lightly floured board until dough measures a little larger than 8 x 12 inches.

Trim off the uneven edges, and use a ruler to mark off 4-inch squares (you should get six). Cut with a sharp knife.

Place 1 rounded tablespoonful of Cream Cheese Filling in the center of each square.

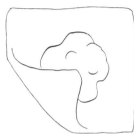

Brush each corner of the pastry with egg wash.

Fold dough over filling diagonally, one corner at a time, forming a pocket that completely encloses the cheese.

Place on a lightly buttered baking sheet, cover loosely with plastic wrap, and allow to proof in a warm place for 1½ hours, until light and about one-third larger in size.

Repeat with second half of dough.

Preheat oven to 350° F.

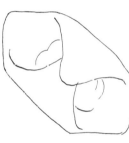

Follow instructions at the end of the "Butter Danish" section (page 18) on baking and glazing.

For Mini–Cheese Danish: We found that in this small size a simple fold-over works better than the pockets.

Cut the rolled out dough into 2-inch squares.

Place one rounded teaspoonful of cheese filling in the center of each square.

Fold the lower left corner up over the filling diagonally.

Brush the top corner with egg wash and then fold it down diagonally over the folded left corner.

Continue with proofing, egg wash, baking, and glazing as indicated at the end of the "Butter Danish" section.

Raspberry Bearclaws

These jam-filled delights can be sprinkled with sliced almonds if you like.

Yield: 12 Danish

½ recipe Basic Danish Dough (page 16), well chilled

RASPBERRY
FILLING

1 cup raspberry preserves
1 cup plain cake crumbs (If you have no leftover cake
crumbs, a store-bought pound cake works well, as do
slightly stale cake-type plain doughnuts.)
½ cup sugar mixed with 1 tablespoon cinnamon

egg wash
½ cup sliced almonds (optional)
Apricot Glaze

Roll out half of dough (keeping remainder wrapped and re-frigerated) on a lightly floured board until it is about 8 x 20 inches.

Spread with up to ½ cup raspberry preserves, spreading evenly and not too thickly.

Sprinkle with ½ cup cake crumbs, patting in gently.

Sprinkle with ¼ cup cinnamon sugar.

Roll up tightly from the wide side, forming a long tube shape with seam on the bottom.

Trim off uneven edges on ends, then cut into 6-inch lengths.

With scissors or a very sharp knife, cut gashes along one side, about ½ inch deep and 1½ inches apart.

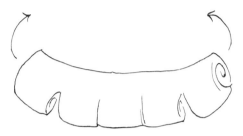

Curve each piece into a horseshoe shape (gashes on the outside edge of the curve) as you place it on a well-buttered baking sheet.

Repeat with other half of dough.

Let rise in a warm place, loosely covered with plastic wrap, until light and about one-third larger.

Follow instructions for egg wash, baking, and glazing given at the end of the "Butter Danish" section (page 18), adding sliced almonds before baking if you wish.

For mini-Danish: Follow instructions above for filling and rolling. Cut into 3-inch lengths. With scissors or a sharp knife, cut gashes along one side about ½ inch deep and 1 inch apart. Place on buttered baking sheet, curving only slightly (these are not big enough to make an actual horseshoe shape). Reduce baking time to about 15 minutes.

Poppy Seed Danish

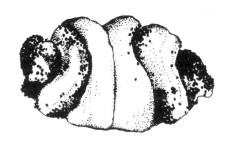

Perhaps the most unusual both in flavor and shaping, our Poppy Seed Danish has an almost butterflylike shape, revealing in each "wing" circles of honey-sweetened filling.

Yield: about 12 Danish

½ recipe Basic Danish Dough (page 16)

POPPY SEED FILLING

½ cup water
½ cup sugar
¼ cup honey
¼ cup butter
1 teaspoon freshly grated lemon rind
1 teaspoon freshly grated orange rind
1½ cups poppy seeds
3 cups plain cake crumbs (If you have no leftovers, use plain pound cake or cake-type doughnuts.)

egg wash
Apricot Glaze

In a heavy saucepan, bring to a boil water, sugar, honey, and butter.

Remove from heat and stir in citrus rinds, poppy seeds, and 2 cups of the cake crumbs.

Cook over low heat, stirring to mix well, until very hot.

Let cool before using. This filling can be made the day before and chilled.

Roll out half of dough (wrapping and chilling the rest) on a lightly floured board to about 10 x 20 inches.

Spread half of cool poppy seed filling in the middle. Spread it toward you all the way down to the bottom long edge, but leave a 1-inch bare border all around the three other sides. The filling should be even and not too thick.

Clockwise from bottom center: Buttermilk Scone (on plate with jam), Cinnamon Swirl Bundt Cake slices, Buttermilk Scone, Irish Soda Bread slices, Blueberry Muffins, Walnut Coffee Cake

Clockwise from bottom center: Cinnamon Danish Swirl, Cinnamon Cigar, Cheese Danish, Poppy Seed Danish, Fruit Fold-over, Raspberry Bear Claw

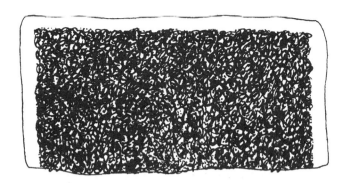

Sprinkle ½ cup cake crumbs over filling.

Brush egg wash on the 1-inch border.

Roll up dough away from you, fairly tight, until you have one long tube with the seam underneath.

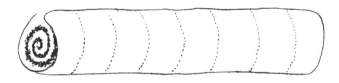

Cut into 2½-inch lengths.

With a wooden spoon handle, press firmly down the center of the cut tube crossways (that is, the handle is parallel to the cut edge of the tube).

As you press down firmly, "wings" will pop out on either side. Pinch the top layer of these wings together a bit in the center to help define the shape (it's OK if they don't stay together).

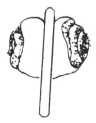

Place on a well-buttered baking sheet and cover loosely with plastic wrap. Let rise in a warm place for 1½ hours or until light and one-third larger.

Repeat with remaining dough.

See instructions on egg wash, baking, and glazing at the end of the "Butter Danish" section (page 18).

Mini-Danish   Roll out one-fourth of the dough only to about 5 x 10 inches. Follow all directions above, cutting the tube into 1½-inch lengths. Repeat three more times. Reduce baking time to about 15 minutes.

Chocolate Cigars

These long, cigar-shaped pastries have a moist filling of semisweet chocolate that is quite irresistible.

Yield: about 12 cigars

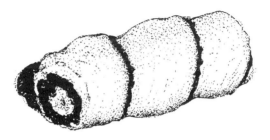

½ *recipe Basic Danish Dough (page 16), well chilled*

CHOCOLATE
FILLING

3 ounces semisweet chocolate
⅓ cup water
1 cup chocolate cake crumbs
1 cup mini–chocolate bits
⅓ cup sugar plus 2 teaspoons cinnamon

egg wash
Apricot Glaze

Chocolate Filling

Prepare a chocolate spread by melting the chocolate and water together in a double boiler and stirring until smooth.

Roll out half the dough (keeping remainder wrapped and chilled) on a lightly floured board to about 10 x 20 inches.

Smooth on half of the chocolate spread with the flat of your hand, covering the dough evenly.

Sprinkle with ½ cup chocolate cake crumbs.

Distribute ½ cup mini–chocolate bits.

Sprinkle with half the cinnamon sugar.

Roll filling in lightly with a rolling pin.

To Shape Cigars   Cut dough into 1½-inch-wide strips.

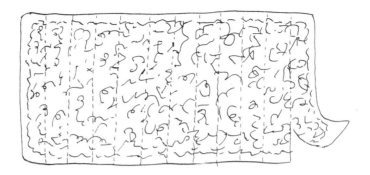

Roll up each strip, starting from the bottom, at an angle toward the right so that the spiral shape is created. After four spiral turns (about 5–6 inches), cut. Push ends in a bit to firm up the shape. You can piece the strips together easily; just keep wrapping up the cigars until they are the right length.

Repeat for remaining dough.

To Bake   Place on well-buttered baking sheet, cover loosely with plastic wrap, and let proof in a warm place until soft and about one-third larger. See end of "Butter Danish" section (page 18) for instructions on egg wash, baking, and glazing.

Mini-Danish   Either cut narrow ¾-inch strips and make little cigars about 3 inches long, or roll up jelly roll fashion and cut 1-inch slices, forming simple chocolate swirls. Decrease baking time to about 15 minutes.

Cinnamon Cigars

A classic combination of cinnamon sugar and almond fills this flaky spiral Danish. Cinnamon Cigars are wonderful with morning or afternoon coffee. Like all Danish, they are best when warmed up gently before serving.

Yield: About 12 cigars

½ recipe Basic Danish Dough (page 16), well chilled

CINNAMON
FILLING

3 egg whites
7 ounces almond paste
1 cup plain cake crumbs
½ cup finely ground almonds (optional)
½ cup sugar plus 1 tablespoon cinnamon

egg wash
Apricot Glaze

Cinnamon Filling

Prepare an almond spread by blending the egg whites and almond paste, a bit at a time, with an electric mixer, until mixture is smooth and of a pastelike consistency. (If you have no almond paste, you can use a mixture of 3 egg whites, 3 tablespoons sugar, and 1 teaspoon almond extract, beaten together until lightly foamy. You could also add a sprinkle of finely ground almonds for extra texture and flavor.)

Roll out half the dough (keeping remainder wrapped and chilled) on a lightly floured board to about 10 x 20 inches.

Smooth on half the almond spread with the flat of your hand, covering the dough evenly.

Sprinkle with ½ cup cake crumbs. Sprinkle with half the cinnamon sugar. Roll the filling in lightly with a rolling pin.

To Shape Cigars

Cut into 1½-inch-wide strips.

Roll up, starting from the bottom, at an angle toward the right so that the spiral shape is created. After four spiral turns (about 5–6 inches), cut. Push ends in a bit to firm up the shape. You can piece the strips together easily; just keep wrapping up the cigars until they are the right length.

Repeat for remaining dough.

To Bake   Place on a well-buttered baking sheet, cover loosely with plastic wrap, and let proof in a warm place until soft and about one-third larger. See end of "Butter Danish" section (page 18) for instructions on egg wash, baking, and glazing.

Mini-Danish   Either cut narrow ¾-inch strips and make little cigars about 3 inches long, or roll up the whole sheet of dough jelly roll fashion and cut 1-inch slices, forming simple cinnamon swirls. Decrease baking time to about 15 minutes.

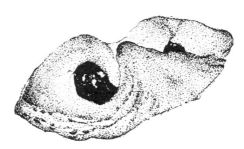

Fruit Fold-overs

We make both apricot and prune Danish with a simple fold-over shaping. The fillings are easily prepared from dried fruits and can be sweetened to taste.

Yield: 12 Danish

½ recipe Basic Danish Dough (page 16)

PRUNE FILLING   *12 ounces pitted prunes*
1 cup water
1 teaspoon grated lemon rind

or

APRICOT
FILLING   *8 ounces dried apricots*
1 cup water
6–8 teaspoons honey

egg wash
Apricot Glaze

Cook all ingredients for fruit filling together over a low flame until very soft, at least 45 minutes.

Mash well with a fork or use an electric mixer to purée, adding additional honey or lemon juice to taste.

Roll dough out on a lightly floured board until a little larger than 8 x 12 inches.

After trimming off uneven edges, cut into 4-inch squares. Moisten two diagonally opposite corners with egg wash. Place 2 tablespoons filling in center of square.

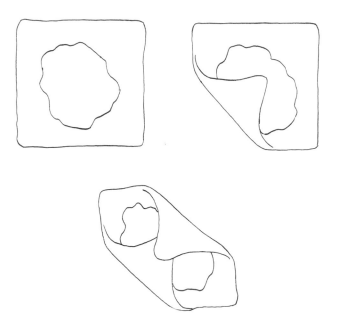

Bring the lower moistened corner up over the filling, then the upper moistened corner over that, overlapping.

Place on well-buttered baking sheet, cover loosely with plastic wrap, and allow to proof for 1½ hours in a warm place. Danish should be soft when touched and be about one-third larger.

Repeat with remaining dough. See instructions at the end of the "Butter Danish" section (page 18) about egg wash, baking, and glazing.

Mini-Danish   Cut 2-inch squares and use only 1 tablespoon filling in the center. Reduce baking time to about 15 minutes.

Cinnamon Raisin Swirls

These are perhaps the easiest Danish to shape—simply roll up and slice, then wait patiently for the yeast to do its work.

Yield: about 12 Danish

½ recipe Basic Danish Dough (page 16)

3 egg whites
7 ounces almond paste
½ cup sugar mixed with 1 tablespoon cinnamon
1 cup raisins
1 cup plain cake crumbs

egg wash
Apricot Glaze

Roll half the dough into a long, fairly narrow rectangle on a lightly floured board to about 6 x 20 inches. Cut off uneven edges. (Wrap and chill the rest of the dough.)

Beat together the egg whites and almond paste with an electric mixer. (If you have no almond paste, you can use a mixture of 3 egg whites, 3 tablespoons sugar, and 1 teaspoon almond extract, beaten together until lightly foamy. You could also add ½ cup of finely ground almonds for extra texture and flavor.)

Spread half of this almond spread with the palm of your hand all over the dough.

Sprinkle with half the cinnamon sugar.

Sprinkle with half the raisins.

Sprinkle with half the cake crumbs.

Use a rolling pin to roll lightly over everything, pressing in the filling slightly.

Roll up tightly as for a jelly roll, starting with the shorter end, forming a 6-inch-long tube with the seam underneath.

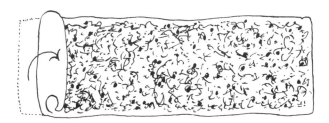

Slice into 1-inch-wide slices. Place on well-buttered baking sheet, pressing down on each one slightly with your palm to flatten it.

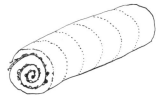

Repeat with remaining dough.

Cover loosely with plastic wrap, and let rise in a warm place for about 1½ hours or until light and at least one-third larger.

Follow the directions for egg wash, baking, and glazing at the end of the "Butter Danish" section (page 18).

Mini-Danish   Proceed as above except roll up from the long side, giving a 20-inch tube, which you then will cut into 1-inch slices. The pastries will be much smaller in diameter and you will get twice as many. Reduce baking time to about 15 minutes.

Hot Cross Buns

A Lenten specialty based on an old English recipe, these fragrant yeast-raised spiced buns are baked with currants and diced citron and finished with the traditional cross of fondant frosting. They take about three to four hours to complete, so perhaps are best baked the day before, but not frosted, and then tightly bagged for storage. The finishing with frosting as well as reheating in a low oven can easily be done in the morning.

Since these buns are definitely a breakfast treat, they are included in this chapter. If you are not accustomed to working with yeast, please read the introduction to the bread chapter for basic principles and techniques.

Yield: 16 buns

> 2 packages dried yeast
> 1 cup very warm water
> ¼ cup light brown sugar
> ¼ cup lightly salted butter, melted
> ⅓ cup milk powder
> 1½ teaspoons salt
> ½ teaspoon ground cloves
> ½ teaspoon ground ginger
> ½ teaspoon ground nutmeg
> ½ teaspoon ground mace
> ½ teaspoon ground cinnamon
> 2 eggs, lightly beaten
> 4 cups unbleached flour
> ½ cup currants
> ½ cup finely diced citron
> egg wash: 1 egg beaten with 2 tablespoons water
> ¾ cup sifted powdered sugar
> 2–3 tablespoons heavy cream

Dissolve yeast in warm water. Add brown sugar, melted butter, milk powder, salt, spices, and eggs. Stir well.

Gradually work in 3 cups of flour, forming a soft, sticky dough. Beat well with a wooden spoon.

Stir in currants and citron, distributing them evenly.

Work in enough remaining flour to make a soft dough that just begins to leave the sides of the bowl and form a ball.

Place in a lightly oiled bowl, turning ball of dough to oil the top. Cover with plastic wrap and set in a warm place to rise until double, about 1½ hours.

Turn onto lightly floured board, punch down, and knead lightly.

Generously butter two large muffin tins.

Form dough into large balls that fill the muffin cups three-quarters full (you could use an ice-cream scoop to get a uniform size, but then hand-shape it into a smooth ball).

Let rise in muffin pans until light and rounded, not quite doubled (about 1 hour).

Preheat oven to 350° F.

Brush with egg wash.

Bake for 20–25 minutes, until golden brown.

Let cool completely before frosting.

Frosting

In a small bowl beat sifted powdered sugar with cream until a thick frosting is formed.

Using a small spoon, run a ribbon of frosting vertically and then horizontally, forming a cross, on top of each cooled bun.

Irish Soda Bread

Although traditional for Saint Patrick's Day, this caraway-seeded and currant-studded crusty loaf is delicious any time of year. Unlike the yeasted breads, it can be made in a little over an hour and is delicious still warm from the oven. The mixing procedure is like that for scones, and it works up quickly and easily, even for the inexperienced bread baker. It is best eaten within a day of baking—and usually disappears before there are any leftovers to worry about.

Yield: 1 round loaf

3 cups sifted unbleached flour
1½ teaspoons baking soda
1½ teaspoons baking powder
½ teaspoon salt
2 ounces (½ stick) lightly salted butter, softened at room
* temperature*
¾ cup currants or raisins
1 tablespoon caraway seeds
1 egg
1 cup buttermilk
2 tablespoons honey

Preheat oven to 350° F.

Thoroughly mix together sifted flour, soda, baking powder, and salt. Cut in soft butter, working it in with your fingers until it is evenly distributed and the texture is a bit like corn meal.

Stir in currants and caraway seeds.

Beat egg, buttermilk, and honey together in a small bowl.

Add milk mixture to dry ingredients, stirring briefly only to moisten evenly. Do not overmix.

Turn onto lightly floured board and briefly knead just to form a smooth dough. Shape into a high, round ball.

Place on buttered baking sheet.

Slash across vertically and horizontally about 4 inches long and ½ inch deep.

Bake at 350° for about 50–55 minutes.

Cool for about 20 minutes before slicing.

2 Crusty Loaves

An Assortment of Hearty Handmade Breads

Greyston Bakery produces a truly wonderful assortment of loaves varying in color, texture, and shape as well as taste. The variety in our bread line was brought home during a sales demonstration at which we were able to admire the whole array as it spilled abundantly from a large bushel basket—dark raisin-studded pumpernickel side by side with golden braided challah and long sesame-sprinkled Italian, whole wheat next to New York sour rye, potato onion rounds leaning against Swedish rye loaves. These are honest handmade breads, baked with the finest flours, with organically grown whole grains, with no preservatives, no bleached flours, no hardened fats, no colorings or other additives. They are truly "staff of life" loaves.

Although you will encounter common techniques and common basic procedures, in the recipes that follow, each bread type quite literally has its own distinctive "feel." Some are dense, others rise light, some get punched down a lot, others are just shaped and proofed. We hope you will discover the uniqueness of these crusty loaves and over time come to savor the whole assortment.

A Note on Procedures

If you are new to bread-baking, it is important to understand the living nature of the dough. In working with yeast—that is, in letting yeast work for you—you must provide a suitable environment: warmth, moisture, and food are essential for the yeast to grow. Moreover, the kneading, punching down, and shaping by your hands develop the elasticity, tension, and eventual tenderness of the texture. In short, bread-baking does require hands-on loving care, time, and attention. We are sure you will find this process rewarding, and the results life-sustaining.

At Greyston Bakery we do not use the "sponge" method, but rather combine all ingredients at once and let our two-armed Swiss mixer with dough hooks go to town. After the initial machine mixing, the dough is allowed to rise on the long, oiled wooden table loosely covered with a plastic sheet. The room is very warm because of the ovens, and after an hour or so the dough is large and fat and about to creep right off the table. The dough is vigorously punched down by hand, expressing all the air, and folded until it once more is a smaller mass (this punching down sometimes happens several times). The dough is then divided into portions by weight and hand-kneaded and shaped in the appropriate way. Finally the dough is placed in a greased loaf pan or on a baking sheet sprinkled with corn meal and set to proof (rise) in the "proof box," a draft-free, very warm cabinet near the oven. Loaves are loaded into the oven by a long wooden paddle, and experienced bakers know just the right moment to pull the hot, brown, fragrant loaves onto cooling racks.

Our experienced bread crew, by examining our first attempts at home-testing bread recipes, were able to analyze the texture and let us know how we were doing: an even, overall crumb structure indicated a bread proofed long enough; a ring of compacted dough along the bottom of the bread pointed to insufficient proofing. For the most part, our early efforts tasted good, but they were lacking the high, light texture of our products. We discovered that we tended not to proof long enough, not to punch down enough, not to knead long enough to get a bread similar to that made in the bakery. Without changing any ingredients, but just modifying (mostly lengthening) the procedures, we were able to turn out wonderful, light, delicious loaves.

In outline, the following procedures are common to all our recipes:

1. Dissolve yeast in very warm (100° F.) water; then add flavorings, such as honey, oil, molasses, or salt. The salt should be added last because otherwise it will interfere with the action of the yeast.

2. Add 2–3 cups of flour and stir the mixture vigorously with a wooden spoon.

3. Knead in the remaining flour by hand. Continue kneading for 10–15 minutes until the dough becomes elastic.

4. Put the ball of dough into a lightly oiled bowl and turn it over so that all sides of the ball are oiled. Then cover the bowl loosely with plastic wrap or a damp dish towel and set it in a warm place for the dough to rise.

5. When the dough is doubled, punch it down and fold it in to re-form the ball. This rising may be repeated again, depending on the recipe.

6. Briefly knead the dough and then cut it into portions and shape it for pans or as free-standing loaves on baking sheets.

7. Butter pans or baking sheets. (Note: Do not oil the pans, or the bread may stick. Butter is better; use it generously.)

8. Loosely cover the shaped loaves with plastic wrap and set them to rise until almost double.

9. Brush on egg wash, make slashes where called for, and sprinkle on seeds.

10. Bake bread in a preheated oven at 350° for around 40 minutes, testing for doneness by tapping the bottom and listening for a hollow sound.

11. Cool loaves on a rack for 1 hour before slicing, 3–4 hours before bagging.

Whole Wheat Bread

Our Whole Wheat Bread is unusually light and tender for a 100 percent whole grain bread. The secret, as we discovered by trial and error, is in the double proofing. This dough is allowed to rise twice before it is shaped for the final proofing. When we skipped this second rising, we got a tasty but much denser loaf. In production we use barley malt for sweetening. We have substituted a small amount of honey, since barley malt may not be easily available to the home baker.

Yield: 2 medium loaves (8 x 4 inches)
plus 8 dinner rolls or 1 large loaf
(9½ x 4 inches) and 1 medium loaf

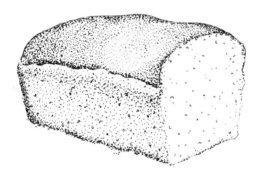 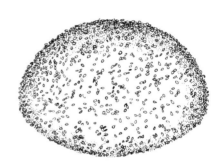

2 packages dry yeast
3 cups very warm water (at about 100° F.)
4 tablespoons honey or barley malt
4 tablespoons soy oil
1 tablespoon sea salt
6 – 7 cups organic stoneground whole wheat flour
½ to ¾ cup sesame seeds for the dough (optional)
egg wash: 1 egg beaten with 2 tablespoons water
⅛ cup sesame seeds for garnish

Dissolve yeast in 3 cups warm water. Add honey, oil, salt, and 3 cups of the whole wheat flour. If you want a sesame crunch and flavor, add optional sesame seeds to the dough.

Clockwise from bottom right: Challah, Whole Wheat Rolls, Challah and Raisin Pumpernickel slices, Whole Wheat Bread slices

Clockwise from bottom left: Swedish Rye, New York Sour Rye, Potato Onion
Bread

Stir vigorously with a wooden spoon until your arm is tired.

Add the additional flour, ½ cup at a time, stirring it in until it is too stiff for the spoon.

Turn onto a lightly floured board and knead, adding flour as needed, until the dough is no longer sticky and begins to leave the board and your hands without much extra flour.

Knead some more (at least 10 minutes), really pushing down hard with the heel of your hand. The dough should be elastic and offer some resistance when you poke it. Form it into a smooth ball.

Place dough in a large oiled bowl, turning it over so that the top has a light coating of oil, which prevents excessive drying out. Cover the bowl with plastic wrap. (In pre-plastic days bakers put a well-wrung-out damp dish towel over the top of the bowl, not allowing it to touch the dough.)

Let dough rise in a warm place, near the stove or in an oven with only the pilot light on, until doubled in size. This will be about 1½ hours for regular yeast and about 45 minutes for the new rapid-rise yeast, depending on how warm a place you provide.

Punch down dough in bowl, releasing all the air, and fold down the sides, re-forming it into a ball.

Once again let it rise until double. This time it will go a little faster.

Butter the pans you have selected.

Punch down dough in bowl, turn onto a very lightly floured board, and cut into pieces according to the size of your pans. You will want a piece of dough that fills the pan a little more than halfway. Set aside any extra for dinner rolls.

Knead each piece for a minute, and pat into a rectangle the length of the pan you have chosen. Roll up tight like a jelly roll into an oblong shape with a smooth top. Seal the seam and ends by pinching them together. Put the long seam face down in the pan. Cover loosely with plastic wrap and again proof in a warm place until not quite double.

Preheat oven to 350° F.

If you are making medium loaves and have some dough left for rolls, form 1½-inch balls. To get a smooth top, push up the dough from underneath with your finger, then stretch and pull the dough down and tuck it into the hole underneath. Pinch the seams together. Place the balls so that they almost touch in a buttered pan. Cover loosely with plastic and let rise in the same way as the bread.

When the dough has almost doubled, brush with egg wash and sprinkle with ⅛ cup sesame seeds.

Bake at 350° for about 40–45 minutes, depending on pan size. The rolls bake for only 25 minutes. The tops should be well browned. Remove one loaf from the pan and tap the bottom. It should not be soft and wet, and should sound hollow.

Let cool on a rack for at least 1 hour before slicing. Do not wrap in plastic bags for at least 3–4 hours, so that no moisture is released in the bag.

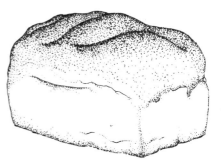

Country White Bread

High-rising and tender, this loaf gets its special flavor and tender texture from freshly cooked mashed potatoes. This is based on a Tassajara Bakery recipe and has many fans on both coasts.

Yield: 2 medium loaves (8 x 4 inches)

1½ cups mashed potatoes (2 medium potatoes)
2 packages dry yeast
2 cups very warm (100° F.) water
3 tablespoons honey
⅓ cup dry milk powder
1 tablespoon salt
3 tablespoons oil
6–7 cups unbleached white or bread flour
egg wash: 1 egg beaten with 2 tablespoons water

Boil 2 medium potatoes until very tender. Drain and mash well with a potato masher until very smooth, adding up to 3 tablespoons hot water. Let cool until warm.

Dissolve yeast in 2 cups very warm water. Add honey, milk

powder, salt, oil, and warm potatoes, stirring well to mix. Gradually add 3 cups flour, stirring vigorously for about 5 minutes.

Add remaining flour ½ cup at a time until dough is too stiff to handle with the spoon.

Turn onto a lightly floured board and knead in enough flour to make a soft but not sticky dough. Knead until elastic and springy (about 10–15 minutes).

Place dough in a lightly oiled bowl, turning to oil the top. Cover loosely with plastic wrap and set in a warm place to rise. Let rise until doubled in volume (about 1½ hours for regular yeast, 45 minutes for rapid-rise yeast).

Punch dough down in bowl, pressing out all the air and turning it to re-form it into a ball. Cover it again with plastic and let rise again; this time it should go a little faster.

Butter bread pans generously.

Punch dough down and turn onto lightly floured board. Divide dough in half and pat each half into a rectangle the length of the pan. Roll up tight like a jelly roll into a rounded oblong. Seal the seam and ends by pinching them together. Put the long seam face down in the pan. Cover lightly with plastic wrap and let rise in a warm place until almost double.

Preheat oven to 350° F.

When dough is almost double, brush with egg wash. With a sharp knife make three parallel diagonal slashes, about ¼ inch deep, across top of dough.

Bake at 350° for 40–45 minutes until dark golden brown, testing for doneness by turning out one loaf and tapping on the bottom, listening for a hollow sound.

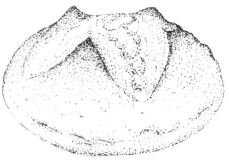

Potato Onion Bread

A Greyston specialty, this high, round, hearth-style loaf is a variation on the Country White Bread that incorporates fresh chopped onion along with the mashed potatoes. It is terrific toasted with grilled cheese or for a real meat-and-potatoes sandwich. At our café we used it as a base for our popular garlic bread. Bring a warm, fragrant loaf to the table with a good soup and a salad for a perfect supper.

Yield: 2 round loaves

1½ cups mashed potatoes (2 medium potatoes)
½–¾ cup finely chopped onion
2 packages dry yeast
2 cups very warm (100° F.) water
3 tablespoons honey
⅓ cup dry milk powder
1 tablespoon salt
3 tablespoons oil
6–7 cups unbleached white or bread flour
egg wash: 1 egg beaten with 2 tablespoons water

Boil 2 medium potatoes in water until very tender. Drain and mash (with skins) with a potato masher until very smooth, adding up to 3 tablespoons hot water. Let cool until warm to the touch.

Chop 1 large onion very finely. Use ½–¾ cup depending on your passion for onion.

Dissolve yeast in 2 cups very warm water, add honey, milk powder, salt, oil, warm potatoes, and onions, stirring well to mix. Gradually add 3 cups flour, stirring vigorously.

Add remaining flour ½ cup at a time until dough is too stiff to handle with a spoon.

Turn onto lightly floured board and knead in enough flour to make a fairly stiff dough that is no longer sticky. Knead until elastic and springy (about 10–15 minutes).

Place dough in a lightly oiled bowl, turning to oil the top. Cover loosely with plastic wrap and set in a warm place to rise. Let rise until doubled in volume (about 1½ hours for regular yeast, 45 minutes for rapid-rise yeast).

Punch dough down in bowl, pressing out all the air and turning to re-form it into a ball. Cover again with plastic and let rise again; this time it should go a little faster.

Butter a large baking sheet.

Punch dough down and turn onto lightly floured board. Divide dough into thirds. Knead each piece, adding a little more flour to make a dough stiff enough to hold a round shape. (You can test this by forming a ball and letting it rest for a few minutes. If it quickly flattens out, it needs more flour.) Repeat with each third of dough.

To shape the loaves, form into a compact ball by first folding dough inward while rotating against the board to form a "mushroom cap" (tucking dough always inward toward the bottom center). The rounded side of the cap is toward you. Repeat this rotation about ten times.

Lay the ball of dough on its side. The bottom is now toward the right. Place your cupped hand on the right-hand third of dough. Skid the dough ball forward with your cupped hand, applying pressure to the front of dough ball. The bottom, after this step, should resemble a whirlpool. This process tightens and firms up the dough and allows a high, round shape. Repeat this skidding about ten times.

Tuck the end underneath, and place ball on buttered baking sheet.

Repeat with remaining dough.

Set to proof in a warm place, lightly covered with plastic wrap.

Preheat oven to 350° F.

When loaves are almost doubled, brush with egg wash.

Slash ¼ inch deep twice, first vertically, then horizontally (about 4 inches long) with a sharp knife, forming a cross in the top. As the bread bakes, this will open up, forming the four points characteristic of this style of shaping.

Bake for 35–40 minutes at 350° until loaf is golden brown and produces a hollow sound when tapped on the bottom.

Let cool for at least 1 hour before slicing, 3–4 hours before bagging.

New York Sour Rye

Testing this one had us worried; most of us thought that the home kitchen could not possibly produce a good sour rye similar to our wonderfully chewy Greyston Bakery version. We were pleasantly surprised that our test kitchen produced an excellent rye bread, even though we did not have the special high-gluten flour used in commercial production. We were also concerned about the sour starter, which turned out to be simple and fuss-free. Although it does need to be made five days before baking the bread, it works beautifully.

Yield: 2 large loaves

SOUR STARTER

½ package dry yeast
1 rounded teaspoon honey
1 cup warm (100° F.) water
1 cup unbleached flour

The starter ingredients should be mixed together in a large jar or plastic container. Leave the mixture unrefrigerated on your kitchen counter, loosely covered. We left a wooden spoon in it to stir it down, and the spoon kept the lid from fitting tightly. The starter has to breathe. Each day stir it down and take a whiff. It should begin to smell sour, but never bad or spoiled, by the fourth day. Use on the fifth day, or cover and refrigerate. Do not keep longer than a week, for best results.

If you plan to bake sourdough bread often, you can replenish the starter and keep it going. To do this, make a double batch of starter and, after using 1 cup in the recipe, replenish the starter by stirring in 1 cup warm water and 1 cup flour. Keep the renewed mixture unrefrigerated 2–3 days until you get that nice sour smell; then cover and store in the refrigerator. This is, so the story goes, how prospectors during the Gold Rush days kept their sourdough going indefinitely.

BREAD

1 cup sour starter
2 cups very warm (100° F.) water
2 packages yeast
1 tablespoon salt
2 tablespoons caraway seeds
2 cups fine rye flour
4–5 cups white bread flour or unbleached white flour
egg wash: 1 egg beaten with 2 tablespoons water

Combine starter, warm water, yeast, salt, caraway, 1 cup rye flour, and 1 cup white flour. Beat very well with wooden spoon. Let stand for about ½ hour to activate starter and yeast.

Add 1 more cup rye flour and as much of the white flour as you can mix in with the spoon. Stir vigorously.

Turn onto a lightly floured board and knead in enough white flour to form a fairly stiff dough. Knead for about 10 minutes, until dough is elastic and springy to the touch.

Place in a lightly oiled bowl, turning to oil top of dough. Let rise in a warm place until doubled in size.

Butter two baking sheets.

Punch down dough and turn onto lightly floured board. Divide dough in half. Work in extra flour if needed to form a dough that will hold its shape in a long free-standing loaf. Knead each piece smooth, pat into a rectangle, and roll up tight as for a jelly roll, forming a long tube with tapered ends. Seal seam and ends by pinching together. Sprinkle corn meal on board and let shaped loaves, seam side down, rest on corn meal. Place loaves on the buttered baking sheets and cover lightly with plastic wrap.

Preheat oven to 350° F.

Let rise until almost doubled. Brush with egg wash and slash diagonally ¼ inch deep three times with a sharp knife.

Bake at 350° for about 35–40 minutes, until golden brown and bread sounds hollow when tapped on bottom.

Let cool on a rack at least 1 hour before slicing, 3–4 hours before bagging.

Swedish Rye

This is a slightly sweet pan loaf, flavored with fresh orange rind, caraway, and sour cream. Its flavor is really brought out by toasting, but it is also a good sandwich bread and lovely with assorted cheeses and fruit for a light meal. Do try this one; it is unusual and rather captivating.

Yield: 2 medium loaves

2 packages dry yeast
2 cups very warm (100° F.) water
½ cup honey
½ cup soy oil
½ cup sour cream
grated rind of 1 large orange
3 tablespoons caraway seeds
1 tablespoon salt
2 cups fine rye flour
4–5 cups unbleached white flour
egg wash: 1 egg beaten with 2 tablespoons water

Dissolve yeast in warm water, adding honey, oil, sour cream, orange rind, 2 tablespoons caraway seeds, and salt. Stir in 2 cups rye flour and 1 cup white flour. Mix very vigorously with a wooden spoon.

Gradually add white flour until dough is too stiff to mix with a spoon.

Turn onto lightly floured board and work in flour until dough is no longer sticky. Knead for about 10 minutes, until elastic and springy.

Place in a lightly oiled bowl and turn to oil top. Cover bowl loosely with plastic wrap and let rise in a warm place until doubled.

Punch down in bowl, then turn onto lightly floured board and divide in half. Knead each piece a little, then pat into a rectangle the length of the pan. Roll up tight, forming a rounded oblong. Place in buttered pan, cover loosely with plastic wrap, and let rise in a warm place until doubled.

Preheat oven to 350° F.

Brush proofed loaves with egg wash and sprinkle with remaining tablespoon of caraway seeds.

Bake at 350° for 40–45 minutes, until loaves are golden brown and sound hollow when tapped on the bottom.

Cool on a rack for 1 hour before slicing, 3–4 hours before bagging.

Challah

Traditionally a Jewish Sabbath bread, this delicious braided loaf has the feathery crumb characteristic of an egg-rich dough and a golden shiny crust sprinkled with poppy seeds. Should you ever have any leftover challah that gets stale, it makes fabulous French toast. We have had quite a few customers order our pan challah just for that purpose. It is not difficult to make and looks quite festive on the dinner table.

Yield: 2 very large braids, either freestanding or in 2 large pans (9 x 4 inches), or 1 large braid and 1 loaf in a medium pan

2 packages dry yeast
2 cups very warm (100° F.) water
½ cup honey
1 tablespoon salt
4 tablespoons soy oil
6 eggs, lightly beaten
7–8 cups unbleached white flour
egg wash: 1 egg beaten with 2 tablespoons water
2 tablespoons poppy seeds (optional)

Dissolve yeast in very warm water, add honey, salt, oil, beaten eggs, and 3 cups flour. Stir vigorously until smooth.

Gradually add more flour until dough is too stiff to work with a wooden spoon.

Turn onto lightly floured board and knead in as much flour as needed to make a fairly stiff dough. Knead for at least 10–15 minutes, until it becomes elastic and springs back when prodded.

Turn into a lightly oiled bowl, turning to oil top. Cover bowl lightly with plastic wrap and set in a warm place to rise until doubled, about 1½ hours.

Punch down in bowl, re-form ball, and let rise again until doubled, about 1 hour.

Turn onto lightly floured board and divide in half. While you work on one half, put rest of dough back in oiled bowl to rest.

To braid the challah, use a simple three-strand braid tucking the ends under for a smooth, rounded finish.

Working with half of dough, divide it into thirds. Roll each piece into a 10-inch-long strand by rolling with the flat of your hand against the board, working from the middle out to the ends. When the strands are all even and round and about the same length, braid them together, stretching slightly as you work down. Turn under both ends, hiding the beginning and end points. Set the braided challahs either on a buttered baking sheet or in a buttered bread pan. Repeat with other half of dough. Cover loosely with plastic wrap and allow to proof until doubled in size, about 45 minutes.

Brush with egg wash and sprinkle with poppy seeds if desired.

Bake at 350° for 40–45 minutes, or until golden and hollow-sounding when tapped on bottom.

Cool on a rack. Wait 1 hour before slicing, 3–4 hours before bagging.

Italian Bread

A simple, straightforward crusty Italian loaf, sprinkled with sesame seeds, this recipe can also be used for small rolls, hero loaves, or a ring-shaped larger loaf. There are two secrets to this bread: one is to incorporate enough flour to make a dough stiff enough to hold its shape in the oven; the second is to place a pan of hot water on the bottom rack of the oven to provide a steamy environment for baking. Some bakeries spray the proofed bread with a fine mist of water, but our bakery oven has a steaming feature, and it seems to work well to develop that characteristic crusty loaf. Italian bread doesn't last long—it is best the day it's baked. It can be stored in a plastic bag, but then that crust will get soft. Just time it right (start the bread right after lunch) and have a fresh, hot loaf ready to serve with your lasagna and salad, and it will disappear very quickly.

Yield: 2 large loaves

2 packages yeast
2 cups very warm (100° F.) water
1 tablespoon sugar
2 tablespoons oil
1 tablespoon salt
6 – 7 cups white bread flour or unbleached white flour
1 egg white beaten with 2 tablespoons water
2 tablespoons sesame seeds

Dissolve yeast in very warm water. Add sugar, oil, salt, and 3 cups flour, and stir vigorously with a wooden spoon.

Add additional flour until dough is too stiff to stir with spoon. Then turn onto a floured board and continue to add flour until a very stiff dough is formed. Knead well (10 – 15 minutes) until elastic and supple.

Turn into a lightly oiled bowl, turning ball to oil top. Cover bowl loosely with plastic wrap and set in a warm place to rise until double. This will take about 1½ hours for regular yeast, 45 minutes for rapid-rise, depending on warmth.

Punch down dough and turn onto lightly floured board, kneading lightly.

At this point you can work in more flour if needed. Shape

dough into a tube and watch whether it sags and flattens out quickly while sitting on the board. If so, it needs a bit more flour. It should be able to hold its tube shape with only a slight release from a round to an oval shape.

Butter a large baking sheet and sprinkle it lightly with corn meal.

Divide dough in half and pat each piece into a long rectangle, about 5 x 16 inches. Roll up tight along the long side, forming a long, narrow tube. Set the tubes on the corn meal–sprinkled baking sheet and let rise in a warm place until doubled.

Preheat oven to 350° F. Set a large roasting pan of hot water on the bottom rack to provide steam.

When the bread has doubled (about 45 minutes to 1 hour), brush with egg white, slash diagonally ¼ inch deep several times, and sprinkle with sesame seeds.

Bake for 35–40 minutes until well browned and hollow-sounding on the bottom.

Let cool for 1 hour before dinner.

Raisin Pumpernickel

A dark, dense loaf with an Old World flavor, our pumpernickel is wonderful with cream cheese and delicious toasted and buttered. In developing this recipe, we were determined not to use artificial caramel coloring to get that dark tone characteristic of pumpernickel. After several experiments, we found that a bit of Postum (a grain beverage) and a little cocoa, plus the molasses used for sweetening, gave just the right shade in a natural and flavorful way. This bread is unusual in that most of the water for the recipe is used first to cook the corn meal. With this corn meal mush as a base, yeast, flavorings, and flours are worked in. The dough will be sticky and very heavy in your hands, but it will eventually respond to kneading in its own dense way. You will find it very satisfying to produce these earthy, well-flavored loaves at home.

Yield: 2 medium round loaves

1¾ cups water
½ cup corn meal (preferably organic stoneground)
2 packages dry yeast
¼ cup very warm (100° F.) water
½ cup molasses
1 tablespoon soy oil
2 teaspoons unsweetened cocoa
2 teaspoons Postum
2 teaspoons salt
1 tablespoon caraway seeds
1 cup whole wheat flour
1 cup fine rye flour
4 cups white bread flour
1 cup raisins
egg wash: 1 egg beaten with 2 tablespoons water

Boil water and pour into a bowl with corn meal. Stir to remove lumps. Let cool for 25 minutes.

Dissolve yeast in ¼ cup very warm water in a large bowl.

When it is just very warm to the touch, but not at all hot, stir the cooked corn meal into the yeast, mixing well. Add molasses, oil, cocoa, Postum, salt, caraway seeds, and whole wheat and rye flours. Stir vigorously with a spoon until your arm is tired. Stir in the raisins.

Gradually add the white flour, ½ cup at a time, until the dough is too stiff to stir with a spoon.

Turn onto a lightly floured board and knead in as much of the flour as needed to make a dough that won't stick to everything. Knead well for 10–15 minutes. The dough should be thick and dense. Place in a lightly oiled bowl, covered loosely with plastic wrap, and let rise until doubled, almost 2 hours, depending on warmth.

Punch down and turn onto floured board, and divide into two equal portions for shaping into "cannonballs." Our bread experts can shape one with each hand simultaneously! It is uncanny. We struggled valiantly to follow their instructions but could only use one hand at a time.

The aim is to form compact balls that will not sag sideways as they bake but will keep their shape pretty well and rise upward during proofing. First, fold the dough inward while rotating it against the table to form a "mushroom cap," always tucking the dough inward toward the bottom center. The rounded side of the cap is toward you, tipped on its side on the table. Repeat this rotation about ten times.

Next, lay the ball of dough on its side so that the bottom is toward the right. Place your cupped hand on the right third of the dough. Skid the dough ball forward with the cupped hand applying pressure to the front of the dough ball. The bottom, after this step, should resemble a whirlpool. This process tightens and firms up the dough and allows a high, round shape. Repeat about ten times. If this procedure seems impossible, shape dough into high, round balls as best you can. The bread will turn out a little flatter but just as tasty.

Tuck the end underneath, and place the ball on a buttered baking sheet sprinkled with corn meal. Repeat with other half.

Cover loosely with plastic wrap and allow to proof until double, about 1–1½ hours.

Preheat oven to 350° F. Brush rounds with egg wash.

Bake pumpernickels for about 40–45 minutes, until they are dark brown and sound hollow when tapped on the bottom.

Seven-Grain Bread

A wonderful, hearty combination of seven whole grains give this loaf an interesting texture and a full-bodied flavor. Like our Whole Wheat Bread, it needs double proofing, which gives it lightness. This multigrain bread is also a multipurpose bread, for it is delicious for breakfast toast, for lunch sandwiches, and with soup and cheese for supper.

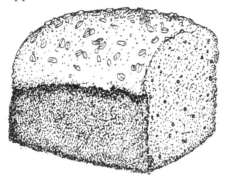

Yield: 2 medium loaves (8 x 4 inches)

⅓ cup millet and ⅓ cup rye chops (coarse rye meal), soaked
*   in hot water to cover*
2 packages dry yeast
2½ cups very warm (100° F.) water
⅓ cup molasses
⅓ cup soy oil
1 cup fine rye flour
⅓ cup corn meal
⅓ cup buckwheat flour
⅓ cup rolled oats
1 tablespoon salt
⅓ cup sesame seeds
4–5 cups whole wheat flour
egg wash: 1 egg beaten with 2 tablespoons water
2 tablespoons rolled oats for topping

Soak millet and rye chops in enough very hot (not boiling) water to cover for 30 minutes. Drain.

Dissolve yeast in very warm water. Add molasses, oil, rye

flour, 2 cups whole wheat flour, and salt. Stir vigorously with a wooden spoon for 5 minutes.

Stir in corn meal, buckwheat flour, and rolled oats, and stir more vigorously.

Add sesame seeds and soaked, drained millet and rye chops. Stir very thoroughly, beating the dough until your arm gets tired.

Gradually add remaining whole wheat flour until dough is too stiff to stir with a spoon.

Turn onto a lightly floured board and knead in sufficient flour to form a dough that can be worked. Knead well for at least 15 minutes until dough is elastic and springs back to your touch.

Form into a ball and place in a lightly oiled bowl, turning dough over to oil top. Cover loosely with plastic wrap and set in a warm place to rise until doubled. This will take about 1½ hours, depending on warmth.

Punch down in bowl, fold dough under to re-form ball, cover bowl with wrap, and let rise again until doubled.

Punch down and turn onto lightly floured board. Divide into two portions, kneading lightly.

Butter two medium bread pans generously.

Shape dough by patting into a rectangle the length of the pan, then rolling up tightly as for a jelly roll, forming a rounded oblong. Place in buttered pan seam side down, cover loosely with plastic wrap, and set to rise in a warm place.

Preheat oven to 350° F.

When almost doubled, brush with egg wash and sprinkle with rolled oats.

Bake at 350° for 40–45 minutes until loaves are well browned and sound hollow when tapped on the bottom.

Clockwise from bottom right: Éclair, Cream Horn, Cream Puff

Clockwise from bottom right: Apple Puffs, Palm Leaves, Fruit Turnovers

3 Sweet Treats

AN ARRAY OF DELICATE PASTRIES

Flaky, delicate, sweet treats all, the Greyston Bakery pastry repertoire encompasses many European regional specialties. Although many of these pastries are not commonly made in the home kitchen, we found it very exciting to master the techniques required to turn out a beautiful assortment of freshly baked treats. The directions are quite detailed, so do read before you plunge in. The Puff Paste is best made and chilled the day before you plan to bake and serve. The Rugelah and Palm Leaves are perfect on an assorted pastry tray for afternoon coffee. The cream- or fruit-filled treats are ideal for dessert or accompanying a good espresso in the evening.

PUFF PASTE

We use this traditional French Puff Paste for Cream Horns, Palm Leaves, and Fruit Turnovers. It could also be used for Napoleons when baked in a rectangular shape and then layered with cold custard and whipped cream. We also include a recipe for Apple Puffs, a perfect special-occasion dessert for the fall apple season. It is best to make this pastry when the day is cool and crisp and your kitchen is not overheated by either the oven or hot, humid summer weather. You need to allow several hours for rolling and turning the dough—a good project when you are busy cooking other items, such as soup or bread. The essential idea in this pastry is to produce a dough with many thin layers of cold butter, which, when baked in a hot oven, expand into a very flaky crust.

Yield: 6 Cream Horns or 12 Palm Leaves

BASIC PUFF PASTE

½ pound sweet butter
2 cups flour
½ cup ice water
dash salt

The first step is to produce soft but very cold butter. To do this, knead ½ pound (1 cup) sweet butter in a bowl under cold running water. This softens the butter but does not melt it at all. When it is soft, quickly knead in 4 tablespoons of the flour. Pat or roll the butter out on a board completely covered with waxed paper or plastic wrap (a marble slab is ideal) to form a rectangle about 8 x 10 inches. Cover with plastic wrap and chill while you mix the dough.

In a large bowl mix together the remaining flour and dash salt. Gradually add ½ cup ice-cold water, mixing with your hands and continuing to knead the dough until it is very smooth. Form into a ball and wrap in plastic wrap or a plastic bag and chill for 15 minutes.

Both butter and dough should now be cold but not too hard to roll. If they have chilled too long, let them sit out for about 15–20 minutes.

Roll out the dough on a lightly floured board into a rectangle about 10 x 22 inches. You may have to stretch and pull a bit, as the dough tends to spring back at this stage.

Place the chilled rectangle of butter at the lower short end of the dough, leaving a 1-inch border all around. Fold the dough down over the butter, pressing the layers together to seal well. You now have a pocket of butter encased in dough; it should measure about 10 x 10 inches.

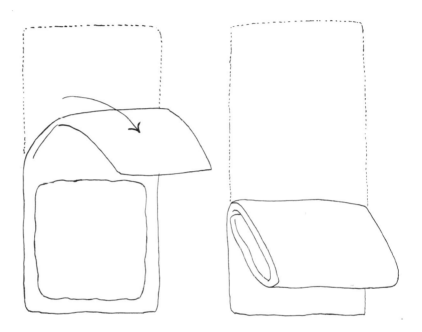

Carefully roll the dough evenly, trying hard not to break the dough or crack the edges. Patch any tears immediately. Roll up and down with the narrow side toward you until it measures 10 x 22 inches again. Fold it toward you into thirds, making sure the corners are even. Pat it lightly together. This is the first turn. Wrap dough well and chill for half an hour. Professionals keep track of the turns by making one shallow finger imprint in the lower right corner of the dough each time they do a turn. You will need to repeat this process six times!

Puff paste can be refrigerated overnight. If you are eager to bake it the same day, let it chill for 1–2 hours after the final turn.

Roll dough thin to 10 x 20 inches and follow shaping, baking, and glazing instructions given in the following recipes.

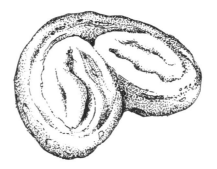

Palm Leaves

Some call these delicate, flaky double spirals "elephant ears"!

Yield: 18–20 pastries

1 recipe ready-to-shape Puff Paste (page 56)
egg wash: 1 egg beaten with 2 tablespoons water
⅓ cup sugar

APRICOT GLAZE

½ cup sugar
½ cup water
3 tablespoons apricot preserves

Preheat oven to 500° F.

Roll dough out to 10 x 20 inches.

Brush rolled-out dough lightly with egg wash.

Sprinkle lightly with sugar (about ⅓ cup).

With the short (8-inch) side toward you, mark the midpoint at about 10 inches along the long side. Draw a line across with a knife—not cutting, just marking. You will be folding the dough, each fold 2½ inches wide, from the top down to that line and from the bottom up to the line, so that you have two flat rolls meeting. Brush the rolls lightly with egg wash.

Turn rolls one on top of the other, and press down gently with your hands along the top, sticking the two rolls together and pressing the dough into an oval shape. Cut off any uneven ends with a sharp knife (you can bake the scraps for snacks).

Slice ½ inch thick with a sharp knife. Place on a lightly buttered baking sheet. At this point they can be frozen. Make sure they are thoroughly spread out on the sheet. After they are frozen, they can be packed in a plastic bag. Defrost thoroughly before baking.

Bake in a very hot (500°) oven for 5 minutes. Then reduce

heat to 350° and bake for 10–15 minutes more, watching carefully, until golden brown.

While pastry is baking, prepare Apricot Glaze by combining glaze ingredients and bringing to a full boil while stirring, then removing from heat.

Brush Palm Leaves with hot glaze and allow to cool.

Cream Horns

These whipped-cream horns are sometimes called "Schiller's Locken," or curls, because of their resemblance to the two long spiral curls favored by the eighteenth-century German writer. Whatever the name, these cornucopia-shaped pastries, sprinkled with sliced almonds, filled with sweetened whipped cream, make an exquisite dessert. Kids always love them and wear impish grins as they bury themselves in cream.

Yield: 6 pastries

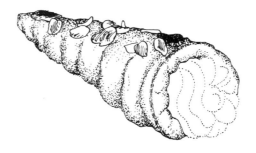

1 recipe ready-to-shape *Puff Paste (page 56)*, rolled out to
 10 x 20 inches
6 metal cone forms, available at gourmet kitchen supply
 shops
egg wash: 1 egg beaten with 2 tablespoons water
½ cup sliced almonds

APRICOT GLAZE
½ cup sugar
½ cup water
3 tablespoons apricot preserves

WHIPPED
CREAM
1 cup heavy cream
¼ cup powdered sugar
½ teaspoon vanilla

¼ cup powdered sugar for dusting

Preheat oven to 500° F.

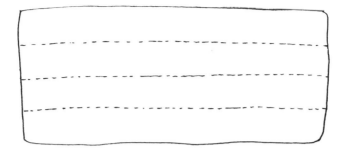

Cut dough into 2-inch strips the long way.

Wrap dough spiral fashion around the metal cones, pressing lightly to seal.

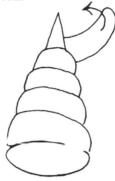

Brush with egg wash and sprinkle with sliced almonds.

Bake in very hot (500°) oven for 5 minutes, then reduce heat to 350° and bake for about 15–20 minutes more, watching carefully.

While horns are baking, prepare Apricot Glaze by combining glaze ingredients and bringing to a full boil while stirring, then removing from heat.

Let cool for a few minutes, then pull out the metal cone.

Brush while warm with hot glaze.

Beat whipped cream ingredients together until thick. Fill cold horns with whipped cream, using a pastry bag with a star tip to press out a swirling flourish at the opening. Alternately, fill with a spoon, ending with a graceful dollop at the wide end of the cone. Dust the pastry with powdered sugar rubbed through a sieve.

Keep refrigerated until served.

Apple Puffs

Essentially baked apples enveloped in maple-syrup-coated flaky pastry, these puffs delight young and old alike. Anyone will rake the leaves for you if you promise an apple puff in return.

Yield: 6 Apple Puffs

1 recipe Puff Paste (page 56)
6 Granny Smith apples, peeled and cored
1 teaspoon cinnamon
¼ cup sugar
¼ cup raisins
egg wash: 1 egg beaten with 2 tablespoons water
½ cup pure maple syrup

While dough is chilling, prepare apples by rolling them in mixture of cinnamon and sugar and filling their centers with 1 teaspoon raisins and 1 teaspoon cinnamon sugar.

Roll out the pastry very thin to a rectangle 14 x 28 inches.

Cut into six 7-inch squares. With a fork, prick each square many times so that steam can escape.

Place a sugared and filled apple in the center of each square.

Brush egg wash on the corners of each square.

Bring up corners together, tucking points deeply into the center of the apple. Spear a toothpick into the center to hold the dough in place.

Put in refrigerator to "relax" the dough for 30 minutes.

Preheat oven to 450° F.

Bake at 450° for 10 minutes, turn oven to 350°, and continue baking for at least 35 minutes.

Brush Apple Puffs generously with maple syrup. Return to hot oven for 1–2 minutes to glaze.

Fruit Turnovers

These flaky triangles filled with fruit are delicious served warm with a scoop of vanilla ice cream. Be sure to let them cool for a good 15 minutes—it's no fun to burn your tongue!

Yield: 6 large turnovers

1 recipe Puff Paste (page 56), ready for final rolling

FRUIT FILLING
*1½ cups fresh or thawed frozen sliced fruit (Anything you
  like in a pie will work well here. We suggest cherry, peach,
  blueberry, or apple-cinnamon.)
2–4 tablespoons sugar (or to taste)
2 tablespoons tapioca (fine granulation)
½ teaspoon cinnamon (optional)
egg wash: 1 egg beaten with 2 tablespoons water*

APRICOT GLAZE
*½ cup sugar
½ cup water
3 tablespoons apricot preserves*

Combine fruit with sugar and tapioca, adding cinnamon if desired. Mix well.

Roll out pastry thinly to a rectangle 12 x 24 inches.

Cut into 6-inch squares. Place 2 rounded tablespoons of fruit filling in the center of each square.

Brush edges of pastry with egg wash. Fold over diagonally, forming a triangle. Press edges to seal with the tines of a fork.

Preheat oven to 450° F. While it is heating, let the pastries rest in the refrigerator for 20 minutes.

Brush lightly with egg wash.

Bake in hot oven for 10 minutes, then reduce oven to 350° and continue baking for 20–25 minutes.

Prepare Apricot Glaze by combining glaze ingredients and bringing to a full boil while stirring, then removing from heat. Brush pastries lightly with hot glaze as they come out of the oven to give them a professional shine.

PÂTE À CHOUX

This cooked egg-rich dough is pressed through a pastry bag to form delicate cream puffs, éclairs, and a fabulous Paris Brest. You will need a medium star tip for the cream puffs and a plain round tip for the éclairs. At Greyston Bakery we make these in fairly large standard sizes, but you might enjoy experimenting with minipuffs and mini-éclairs to add to an assortment of sweets for an elegant event. These can all be made without a pastry bag. For the cream puff, a large dollop can be spooned onto the baking sheet, topped with a smaller dollop for a rising crown. Éclairs can be hand-formed if you butter your fingers, but it's a bit tricky (and sticky). This dough also lends itself well to savory fillings for hors d'oeuvres and can make beautiful little puffs to hold a scoop of such everyday spreads as chicken, egg, or tuna salad. Unlike some of the other butter-layered recipes in this chapter, this one is fast and easy and gives very professional results.

Yield: 6 cream puffs or
éclairs; 1 Paris Brest

PÂTE À CHOUX	*1 cup milk*
	⅓ cup lightly salted butter
	1 cup sifted flour
	4 eggs
GRAND MARNIER CUSTARD	*1½ cups milk*
	½ cup sugar
	4 tablespoons flour
	dash salt
	2 egg yolks
	1 tablespoon Grand Marnier or 1 teaspoon orange extract
WHIPPED CREAM FOR PARIS BREST OR CREAM PUFFS	*1 cup heavy cream*
	¼ cup powdered sugar
	½ teaspoon vanilla
CHOCOLATE GLAZE FOR ÉCLAIRS	*3 ounces semisweet chocolate*
	2 ounces (½ stick) sweet butter

Preheat oven to 400° F. for at least 20 minutes.
Let eggs be at room temperature for about 1 hour.
In a heavy saucepan, bring milk and butter to a boil.

Dump in the flour and stir rapidly with a wooden spoon until it becomes smooth and dry and no longer clings to the side of the pan. Remove from heat.

Crack in the eggs, one at a time, beating well to incorporate each egg completely. Keep beating vigorously until the dough loses its slippery quality. Fill pastry bag, using star tip for cream puffs or round tip for éclairs. Lightly butter a baking sheet.

Press out the puffs (literally "cabbages," or *choux* in French) by holding the pastry bag upright close to the baking sheet, squeezing out the paste without moving the bag. For the éclairs you move the tube along for about 4 inches while pressing evenly. In both cases you finish with an upward reverse motion.

Bake in the hot oven for 10 minutes, then reduce the heat to 350° and bake for 20–25 minutes longer.

Cool before filling. Split puffs open and press the filigree of pastry to the sides of the shell to create hollowed-out cases.

To Prepare Custard	Heat milk to scalding (just below a boil) and remove from heat.

Combine sugar, flour, dash salt, and egg yolks in the top of a double boiler set over hot water. Stir this well; it will become light. Gradually stir in hot milk until blended. Cook, stirring continuously, until mixture is about to boil. Then lift it off the hot water. Stir in the Grand Marnier liqueur or extract.

Keep stirring to help custard cool down. Then chill completely, setting the saucepan in a bath of ice water and then in the refrigerator, well covered with plastic wrap. Be sure the custard is cold before using.

To Assemble Cream Puffs

Cut the shell in half horizontally. Fill the bottom half of each puff with approximately 2 tablespoons cold custard. Beat together whipped-cream ingredients. Then fill the pastry bag with whipped cream and squeeze concentric circles of cream over the custard, working from the inside out, letting the cream artfully overhang the shell. Alternatively, spoon a large dollop of whipped cream over the custard. Replace top of puff and dust with powdered sugar rubbed through a sieve. Refrigerate until served.

To Assemble Éclairs

Cut in half horizontally. Fill with about 3–4 tablespoons custard and replace top. Melt butter and chocolate together in a double boiler over hot water, stirring until smooth. Pour this glaze while warm over the filled éclairs, letting it drip down the sides and hide the incision. Refrigerate until served.

Paris Brest

A mouth-watering, airy confection, the Paris Brest is created with a large ring of Pâte à Choux filled with chocolate mousse and whipped cream.

Yield: 6 servings

1 recipe Pâte à Choux (page 64)
½ cup sliced almonds

CHOCOLATE
MOUSSE

1 cup heavy cream
⅓ cup powdered sugar
⅓ cup unsweetened cocoa powder

WHIPPED
CREAM

1 cup heavy cream
¼ cup powdered sugar
½ teaspoon vanilla

Preheat oven to 425° F.

Spoon the Pâte à Choux onto a buttered baking sheet, carefully forming an 8-inch ring, using all the dough. Sprinkle with sliced almonds. Bake for 15 minutes at 425°, then turn oven to 350° and bake for about 60 minutes longer. Cool and split, removing enough doughy filaments to create a cavity for the mousse and whipped cream.

Prepare Chocolate Mousse by beating all ingredients together in the small bowl of a mixer until thick and holding peaks. Prepare whipped cream by combining all ingredients and beating until thick.

Fill bottom half of shell with chocolate mousse. Top with whipped cream, pressed through a bag or spooned on. Cover with top of shell, and dust lavishly with powdered sugar rubbed through a sieve. Refrigerate until served.

CREAM CHEESE PASTRY

This is a rich, flaky, easy-to-handle pastry with great versatility. We use it mostly for Rugelah and for delicious Mincemeat Turnovers during the holiday season. Incidentally, you can always divide the filling recipes in half and then make two varieties of Rugelah from one batch of dough. This pastry can also be used for vegetable or meat fillings for very impressive hors d'oeuvres or as a main-dish pastry.

1 cup cream cheese at room temperature
1 cup lightly salted butter at room temperature
2 tablespoons powdered sugar
1 teaspoon vanilla extract
dash salt
2¼ cups flour

Let butter and cream cheese soften at room temperature for several hours. Then cream them together until you cannot distinguish one from the other.

Mix in sugar, vanilla, and salt.

Gradually stir in flour, forming a ball of dough that holds together. You may use your hands toward the end, but do so sparingly. Too much kneading toughens the dough.

Wrap dough in plastic and chill for 1–2 hours. If you chill it overnight, remove it from refrigerator at least an hour before you are ready to begin rolling and filling.

Raisin or Cinnamon-Walnut Rugelah

Yield: 3–4 dozen

1 recipe Cream Cheese Pastry (page 67)
1 egg white
1 tablespoon sugar
1 teaspoon almond extract
½ cup sugar plus 1 tablespoon cinnamon
1 cup raisins
1½ cups finely chopped walnuts
egg wash: 1 egg yolk beaten with 2 tablespoons water

Preheat oven to 350° F.

Roll out half the dough into an 8 x 20-inch rectangle on a lightly floured board.

Lightly beat together with a fork the egg white, sugar, and almond extract.

Spread half of the egg white mixture over the rolled-out dough.

Sprinkle with ¼ cup cinnamon sugar.

Distribute ½ cup raisins and ½ cup finely chopped walnuts, and press in lightly with hands.

Roll up tightly, starting with the wide side, forming a long "snake."

Brush the top with egg wash and sprinkle with about ¼ cup walnuts, pressing them on lightly.

Cut into 1½-inch-long rolls.

Place on buttered baking sheet and bake at 350° for about 15–20 minutes, or until golden brown.

Repeat with other half of dough.

Alternatively, make the recipe with only cinnamon sugar and walnuts, omitting the raisins.

Raspberry or Apricot Rugelah

Yield: 3–4 dozen

1 recipe Cream Cheese Pastry (page 67)
½ cup finely chopped walnuts
1 cup raspberry or apricot preserves
egg wash: 1 egg beaten with 2 tablespoons water

Preheat oven to 350° F.

Roll out half the dough to an 8 x 20-inch rectangle on a lightly floured board. Spread thinly with ½ cup preserves.

Roll up tightly starting from the wide side.

Brush with egg wash and sprinkle with ¼ cup finely chopped nuts. Cut into 1½-inch pieces.

Bake on a buttered sheet at 350° for 15–20 minutes until golden. Repeat with other half of dough.

Mincemeat Turnovers

An unusual yet very easy-to-make holiday delicacy.

Yield: 36 turnovers

1 recipe Cream Cheese Pastry (page 67)
1 recipe Mincemeat Filling (page 98)
egg wash: 1 egg beaten with 2 tablespoons water and
  1 teaspoon sugar

Preheat oven to 350° F.

Roll out half the dough to a 9 x 18-inch rectangle on a lightly floured board. Cut into 3-inch squares.

Brush edges with egg wash.

Place scant tablespoon mincemeat just below midpoint of square. Fold in half diagonally, forming a triangle.

Press edges together with the tines of a fork.

Brush with egg wash.

Bake at 350° for about 20 minutes or until golden.

Repeat with other half of dough.

Left to right: Assorted Rugelah and Paris Brest

Clockwise from bottom right: Almond Butter Cookies in assorted shapes, Lace Cookies, Maple Pecan Crisp, Scotch Orange Shortbread Swirl, Linzer Tart, Mocha Kahlúa Brownies

4
Cookies by the Dozen

Short and sweet, Greyston Bakery Cookies are known for their buttery texture and natural flavors. The shortbread and butter cookies, especially if shaped with a cookie press, can be made into exquisite miniatures for the most elegant tea or luncheon. Others, especially our drop cookies filled with chocolate chunks or crunchy with roasted peanuts, will please the football and lunch box crowd. Many of these recipes are perfect for holiday entertaining and giving, and will make unusual additions to your repertoire of homemade specialties.

All these cookies are made faster using an electric mixer, which enables you to cream the butter well, even if it is not soft enough to start with, and to have a batch ready for the oven in no time. Except for the macaroons, all are baked in a moderate oven (350°), which should always be preheated. Letting the hot cookies sit on the sheets for a minute or two before sliding them off to a cooling rack prevents breakage. Always store cookies in a tightly covered container. With the exception of macaroons, all these cookies freeze well if wrapped airtight.

Scotch Orange Shortbread

The recipe for this basic shortbread dough was a gift from the Tassajara Bakery in San Francisco. At Greyston Bakery it is used in three distinct ways: pressed in a swirl for Scotch Orange Shortbread cookies, rolled and cut for Linzer Tarts or other holiday rolled sugar cookies, and rolled thin for a crust for our pecan and fresh fruit tarts. It handles well, keeps for a week in the refrigerator, and always wins compliments for its buttery, not-too-sweet taste. Especially during the holidays, this dough is wonderful to have ready and waiting for cutting out in fancy shapes, for making a dessert shell (to be baked with a filling or baked unfilled and then lined with custard and fresh fruit or your own chiffon filling), or for slicing as a refrigerator cookie into thin butter wafers should you want something fresh from the oven when friends drop in.

Yield: 3 dozen large cookies

**BASIC
SHORTBREAD
DOUGH**

1 cup (½ pound) lightly salted butter at room temperature
½ cup powdered sugar
1 teaspoon orange extract (or 1½ teaspoons for a pronounced orange flavor)
2 cups sifted cake flour
4 ounces pecan halves for centers

Preheat oven to 350° F.

Cream softened butter with powdered sugar until well blended.

Add orange extract to butter-sugar mixture and stir well to incorporate.

Stir in sifted flour one cup at a time, mixing well.

Shape according to one of the variations given below.

Bake for about 15 minutes at 350° until color turns a pale gold. Smaller sugar cookies may take only 12 minutes; larger cookies take longer.

Scotch Orange Shortbread Swirls

Press through a cookie press using a star tip or other desired shape. Press a pecan half in the center.

Shortbread Cut-outs

Chill dough, well wrapped in plastic wrap, for 2 or more hours before rolling. Roll on a lightly floured board about ¼ inch thick and cut as desired:

1. Cut into 2-inch circles. Press pecan half in center.

2. Cut into fancy holiday shapes, brushing lightly with water and sprinkling with colored sugar before baking.

Note: We make our own colored sugar crystals using turbinado sugar (a form of "raw" sugar), which we shake in a jar with a few drops of food coloring. This is our one use of colorings, and we do this just to add sparkle to our holiday cookies.

Shortbread Tart Shells

See page 92.

Linzer Tarts

These European specialties are extra-special when made with our buttery short-bread. Essentially a sandwich cookie filled with fruit preserves and lavishly dusted with powdered sugar, our Linzer Tarts are easily made with our basic shortbread recipe. They melt in your mouth and, if eaten too hurriedly, leak jam on your hands and powder your shirt with sugar. Their deliciousness is definitely worth the mess. In both assembling and eating these, go slowly. Rushing only makes the cookie crumble.

Yield: 8–10 tarts

Basic Shortbread Dough (page 72), chilled 2 hours or longer
raspberry and/or apricot preserves
½ cup powdered sugar

Preheat oven to 350° F.

Roll out dough on lightly floured board with floured rolling pin until about ¼ inch thick. Cut with 2-inch round cutter (scalloped is nice) and place on ungreased baking sheet.

Cut out small center circle with 1-inch or smaller cutter in half of the cookies. (Reroll scraps as you go.)

Bake at 350° for about 12 minutes, until pale golden and edges are starting to brown.

Cool completely on a wire rack at least half an hour.

Place all the tops (with inner circles cut out) close together on a sheet of waxed paper.

Dust sifted powdered sugar thickly over the tops.

Place all the bottoms on another sheet of waxed paper.

Spread 2 teaspoons preserves very carefully on each bottom cookie. Spread evenly, leaving a ¼-inch rim without preserves around the outer edge. Spread the preserves without picking up the cookie; use a flat butter knife and work right on the waxed-paper-covered surface.

Top each preserve-covered bottom cookie with a sugared top cookie, lightly holding it at the edges. Carefully transfer cookies to a serving plate. Do not try to stack these or store them for very long. The basic cookies could be packed and frozen, but the assembled Linzer Tarts should be made the day they are to be served.

Maple Pecan Crisps

Thin, crisp, and not too sweet, this unusual cookie is sweetened only with pure maple syrup. The recipe came to us from the People's Bakery in Minneapolis. These generous people shared their recipes and baking know-how with us during our initial research-and-development phase in 1982. Our version of this recipe, slightly different from the original, is very simple and straightforward: butter, maple syrup, flour, and pecans. If you prefer unrefined ingredients, you can substitute whole wheat pastry flour for the unbleached white. Greyston Bakery sells lots of these crisps to fine health food stores as well as to gourmet shops.

An electric mixer is especially helpful for this recipe.

Yield: 3 dozen 2-inch cookies

1 cup lightly salted butter at room temperature
¾ cup pure maple syrup
2¼ cups unbleached white flour
1 cup pecan pieces

Preheat oven to 350° F.

Cream soft butter, gradually pouring in the syrup and mixing at medium speed with electric mixer until uniform and smooth.

Stir in flour, starting at low speed, 1 cup at a time, until blended. Fold in pecan pieces by hand.

Chill dough for at least 2 hours, well covered with plastic wrap. (It helps to lightly oil a smaller bowl to use for chilling the dough.)

Roll quite thin on a well-floured board with a floured rolling pin. The dough seems to handle best in small amounts, say one-quarter of the dough at a time. Cut with a 2-inch round cutter and place on ungreased baking sheets.

Bake at 350° for about 12 minutes. The cookies should just be changing to a golden light tan. Cool on a rack. Store in a tightly covered container. These freeze well.

Variations

1. Cut dough with a 1-inch round cutter for delicate tea cookies.

2. Use dough for drop cookies (do not chill dough for these). Press a pecan half into the center of each.

Macaroons

Golden macaroons, a Tassajara Bakery original, have been one of Greyston Bakery's very popular products. We add pure wildflower honey, use a special "macaroon shred" of unsweetened dried coconut, and hand-press them in elegant swirls with a pastry bag. We make macaroons in lots of ways: large (macs) and small (minimacs), plain or mixed with cocoa (cocomac and coco-minimac), dipped in bittersweet chocolate (cho-mac, cocho-mac, minicho, minicocho), and sandwiched together with chocolate glaze in the middle (macwich or cocomacwich). The nomenclature may be thoroughly confusing, but the product is indisputably delicious.

The effort to translate our bakery recipe into a home kitchen version has been very difficult for the macaroons, primarily because the kind of coconut shreds we use are not available to the retail customer. The closest approximation comes from the health food store in the form of unsweetened dried coconut. We have made these cookies with the canned sweetened coconut available in supermarkets and, by reducing the sugar in the recipe by half, made a macaroon that was well liked. It wasn't very similar to the Greyston Bakery macaroon in appearance or taste, but it was good.

Unlike all our other cookies, these are not butter-based. Essentially a meringue cookie, they require an electric mixer to whip the egg whites to stiff peaks. They need a well-buttered cookie sheet (or parchment) and a 375° oven. Baking these macaroons in humid, hot summer weather tends to result in a sticky cookie; cool, dry days are best. Finally, these macaroons do not like to be frozen or even refrigerated, but they store well in a tin.

We offer you two versions, our regular bakery macaroon and one substituting potato starch or matzo cake meal for the flour to use during Passover.

Yield: 3–4 dozen medium macaroons

2 egg whites
½ cup sugar
3 tablespoons honey
1 teaspoon almond extract
1 teaspoon vanilla extract
⅓ cup unbleached flour or potato starch or matzo cake meal
3 cups unsweetened dried coconut

Preheat oven to 375° F.

Beat egg whites until starting to expand but still soft.

Add sugar, honey, and extracts.

Beat at high speed until very stiff peaks form (about 8–10 minutes).

Fold in flour (or matzo meal) and coconut by hand.

Drop on well-buttered baking sheets by heaping teaspoonfuls, or use a pastry bag with a star tip #2.

Bake at 375° for about 10 minutes or until golden.

Let cool for a minute, then carefully remove to a rack to cool.

Variations

1. For cocomacs, add 1 additional tablespoon honey to egg white. Then fold in ½ cup unsweetened cocoa with the flour (or matzo meal).

2. Dip the bottoms of cooled macaroons in melted semisweet chocolate, drying upside down on a rack.

3. Sandwich two dipped macaroons together to make a "macwich."

4. If you can only find sweetened coconut, reduce the amount of sugar in the recipe to ¼ cup.

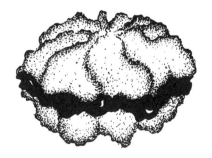

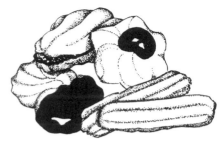

Almond Butter Cookies

These delicate tea cookies are best made with a cookie press, but they can also be made as drop cookies or chilled and rolled out for holiday shapes.

Yield: 4 dozen small pressed cookies

¾ cups (1½ sticks) sweet butter
¾ cup granulated sugar
1 egg yolk
1 teaspoon vanilla extract
1 teaspoon almond extract
4 cups sifted flour
8 ounces semisweet chocolate (optional)

Preheat oven to 350° F.

Cream softened butter.

Mix in sugar thoroughly.

Beat in egg yolk, and extracts until light and fluffy.

Stir in flour by hand, 1 cup at a time, making a soft dough. Do not chill if you are using a cookie press.

Press cookies out, following directions for your cookie press, onto ungreased cookie sheets. We make "fingers," S-swirls, stars, and shells. Bake 8–10 minutes (depending on size) at 350°. Let cool completely on a rack.

Melt 8 squares of semisweet chocolate over hot (not boiling) water in small saucepan or stainless bowl. When melted, remove from flame but leave it over the hot water.

Dip each cookie in chocolate, resting it on a long-tined fork. It can be half-dipped or bottom-dipped, or however you choose. Let set upside down on rack or waxed paper. It helps set the chocolate if you place the dipped cookies in the refrigerator for about 15 minutes. The chocolate should remain solid at room temperature, although a hot summer day might soften it enough to give everyone sticky fingers; in that case, store in the refrigerator in a cookie tin until serving time.

Mocha Kahlúa Brownies

These frosted fudgy confections were developed for the Christmas catalogue of one of our exclusive customers who are chocolate connoisseurs. If you are a chocolate devotee, this recipe is guaranteed to become a favorite.

Yield: 16 small brownies

8 ounces semisweet chocolate
¼ cup butter
3 eggs
½ cup sugar
1 tablespoon instant coffee
1 tablespoon hot water
½ cup flour
½ cup chopped walnuts (optional)

Preheat oven to 350° F.

Melt chocolate and butter over hot water in double boiler. Remove from heat and let cool slightly.

Beat eggs and sugar in small bowl of electric mixer until very light and lemon-colored.

Dissolve instant coffee in water and add to egg mixture.

Stir in melted chocolate mixture. Blend at low speed.

Fold in flour. Mix well at low speed. Stir in nuts by hand.

Pour into buttered and floured 9-inch square pan.

Bake for 20–25 minutes at 350°. Frost when cool. (If desired, sprinkle with coffee liqueur before frosting.)

FROSTING

2 ounces melted semisweet chocolate
½ cup sweet butter
1 cup powdered sugar
1 tablespoon Kahlúa liqueur (or coffee extract)

Melt chocolate over hot water. Let cool slightly.

Cream butter and powdered sugar.

Stir in melted chocolate and Kahlúa or extract.

Spread onto cooled brownies. Let set in a cool place for 30 minutes. Cut brownies into 16 small squares.

All-American Brownies

We developed our brownies (and goldies, too) for Wall Street sidewalk vendors and for brokers and investors rushing to and from the exchange. They are particularly easy to make because we use cocoa rather than melted baker's chocolate, which saves steps and pot-washing. An electric mixer makes this recipe with ease, but a strong arm will do the job just fine. The brownies can be cooled right in the pan (and wrapped and stored in the pan if desired). They keep well if tightly wrapped and also freeze well. At our café we love to serve a "Brownie All the Way," a brownie with a scoop of ice cream, homemade fudge sauce, and fresh whipped cream, topped with chopped walnuts. Of course, they are delicious plain, too.

Yield: 12 brownies

1 cup lightly salted butter at room temperature
1 cup sugar
10 tablespoons unsweetened cocoa
2 eggs, lightly beaten
½ cup unbleached flour, sifted
½ cup chopped walnuts

Preheat oven to 350° F.

Cream butter with sugar until well incorporated.

Mix in beaten eggs until blended.

Add cocoa gradually (otherwise, if you are using a mixer, you might inhale a cloud of cocoa dust).

Stir in flour until well mixed in.

Turn batter into well-buttered, well-floured pan (10¾ x 7 inches or 9 x 9 inches).

Sprinkle walnuts evenly on the top.

Bake for 25 minutes at 350°. When brownies are done, a toothpick inserted in the center will come out clean, and there is slight shrinkage from the sides of the pan.

Cool for at least half an hour before cutting into 12 squares. Make sure these are completely cool before wrapping for storage.

Glorious Goldies

Sometimes called blondies or blond brownies, these favorites are essentially a chocolate-chip cookie bar. Their thickness gives them a wonderful chewy texture. Studded with chocolate chips and nuts, they are quite irresistible! They pack well for picnics or lunch boxes, freeze well, and keep for several days if tightly wrapped.

Yield: 12 bars

¾ cup lightly salted butter at room temperature
½ cup granulated sugar
1 cup light brown sugar
2 eggs, lightly beaten
1 teaspoon vanilla extract
2 cups unbleached flour, sifted
1 cup semisweet chocolate chips or chocolate chunks
1 cup chopped walnuts

Preheat oven to 350° F.

Cream butter and sugars with either a big wooden spoon or an electric mixer.

Mix in lightly beaten eggs and vanilla.

Add flour gradually, mixing well.

Stir in by hand ¾ cup of the chocolate chips or chunks and ¾ cup of the walnuts.

Spread in well-buttered pan (10¾ x 7 inches).

Sprinkle top with reserved chocolate chips or chunks and nuts.

Bake at 350° for about 30–35 minutes. Test for doneness with a toothpick.

Cool for at least 30 minutes before cutting into 12 bars.

DROP COOKIES

At an interfaith conference at Saint Benedict's Monastery in Snowmass, Colorado, leaders of that Cistercian monastery discussed with Bernard Glassman Sensei the question of right livelihood. Drawing on a long history in both the Catholic and Buddhist traditions of working to support their monasteries, they decided to embark on a joint livelihood project, loosely called the Ecumenical Cookie Project. This would not only allow Greyston Bakery to share its baking experience and expertise with the monks of Saint Benedict's and increase its base of support, but also would allow the exchange of monks between the two communities, bringing to life the ecumenical vision of shared work, practice, and study. The plan is to jointly develop recipes, and then for the Colorado location to distribute in the West, the New York location in the East. The cookies are to be made with the finest natural ingredients, packaged, and labeled as the joint livelihood of the Cistercian monks of Snowmass and the Zen Community of New York. The project is still on the back burner, but recipes have been developed by two young monks, one Cistercian from Colorado, one Buddhist from Riverdale (and both, incidentally, named Charlie).

The following seven recipes for drop cookies are home-kitchen versions of these cookies. They all are made by the same basic technique: creaming butter and brown sugar, adding liquids (usually egg and extracts), stirring in flour and nuts, and baking at 350° for 12 minutes. All are easy to make, and several of the recipes are quite unusual variations on typical cookie-jar favorites.

Chocolate Chunk Cookies

Our variation of the well-loved Toll House cookie never fails to please. In our commercial operation we need to have a fairly sturdy cookie that will handle easily and not break in transit. This is a thinner, more delicate cookie. (If you are packing them to send off to a starving student, you might add ¼ cup more flour.) In any case, they are guaranteed to disappear, probably before they are even cooled!

Yield: 4 dozen medium cookies

½ cup lightly salted butter at room temperature
½ cup light brown sugar
¼ cup granulated sugar
1 egg, lightly beaten
1 teaspoon vanilla extract
½ teaspoon baking soda
1 cup all-purpose flour, sifted
½ cup broken nut pieces (walnuts or pecans or macadamias)
4 ounces semisweet chocolate, cut into chunks

Preheat oven to 350° F.

Cream butter and sugars, with an electric mixer if possible.

Add egg and vanilla. Mix completely.

Stir in flour and baking soda until well incorporated.

Chop semisweet chocolate into chunks with strong kitchen knife. Each chunk should be about ½ inch square.

Break nuts into pieces by hand into measuring cup.

Fold in chocolate chunks and nut pieces by hand.

Drop on ungreased cookie sheets by rounded teaspoonfuls, allowing room for cookies to spread.

Bake at 350° for about 12 minutes or until pale brown. Cool for a minute or two on the sheet before removing to a rack to finish cooling.

Chocolate Fudge Drops

A chocoholic's dream, especially in the variations filled with chunks of bittersweet or white chocolate. These cookies mix up easily with an electric mixer but need a bit of care in removing them from the baking sheet, as they are quite thin.

Yield: 3½ dozen medium cookies

¾ cup sweet butter at room temperature
1 cup packed light brown sugar
¾ cup granulated sugar
1 egg, lightly beaten
1 teaspoon vanilla extract
1 cup unsweetened cocoa
scant ¼ cup water
⅛ teaspoon baking soda
½ cup all-purpose flour

Preheat oven to 350° F.

Cream butter with sugars until well blended.

Add egg and vanilla, beating until light.

Alternately add cocoa and water with mixer on low speed (to avoid getting a puff of cocoa powder in your face).

Stir in baking soda and flour until just incorporated.

Drop by teaspoonfuls on well-buttered baking sheets.

Bake at 350° for 12–15 minutes, watching for slightly brown edges.

Cool on sheet for about 3–4 minutes, then carefully remove to rack. If cookies get too hard, return to the oven for a minute or two to soften.

Variations

1. Add 6 ounces chopped bittersweet or white chocolate chunks.

2. Substitute 1 teaspoon mint extract for the vanilla.

3. Add 1 cup broken walnut pieces.

Maple Nut Cookies

These sweet and nutty drop cookies add both real maple syrup and pure maple extract to the brown-sugar-and-butter base. If you want to bake with unrefined ingredients, whole wheat pastry flour (not bread flour) can be substituted for the unbleached white flour.

Yield: 3½ dozen medium cookies

1 cup lightly salted butter at room temperature
1 cup packed light brown sugar
1 egg
⅓ cup pure maple syrup
1 teaspoon vanilla extract
2 teaspoons maple extract
2 cups unbleached flour, sifted
½ teaspoon baking powder
2 cups (8 ounces) coarsely broken pecans or walnuts

Preheat oven to 350° F.
Cream soft butter and brown sugar.
Beat in egg, syrup, and extracts until light and fluffy.
Stir in by hand the sifted flour and baking powder.
Fold in nuts.
Drop by rounded teaspoonfuls onto ungreased baking sheet.
Bake for 12 minutes at 350°.

Oatmeal Raisin Cookies

Our version of this old-fashioned cookie-jar favorite is chewy with lots of whole-some oats and studded with walnuts and raisins.

Yield: 3½ dozen medium cookies

1 cup well-packed brown sugar
1 cup lightly salted butter at room temperature
1 egg, lightly beaten
1 tablespoon water
1 teaspoon vanilla extract
½ teaspoon ground cinnamon
½ teaspoon baking powder
1 cup all-purpose unbleached flour
3 cups old-fashioned rolled oats
½ cup raisins
½ cup coarsely chopped walnuts

Preheat oven to 350° F.

Cream soft butter with brown sugar.

Add lightly beaten egg, water, and vanilla. Mix well.

Add cinnamon, baking powder, and flour, stirring by hand.

Fold in oats, raisins, and nuts. Blend thoroughly to distribute evenly.

Drop by rounded teaspoonfuls on lightly buttered baking sheets.

Bake for 12 minutes at 350° or until light tan.

Clockwise from bottom center: Macwich, Macaroons dipped in semi-sweet chocolate, Macaroon

All-American Brownies and Glorious Goldies

Chunky Peanut Butter Cookies

These are great after school with a glass of milk. They also pack well for take-along treats. We put in lots of roasted peanuts and use a natural (not hydrogenated), lightly salted peanut butter. Adding the nonfat dry milk powder increases the nutritional value of this already high-protein cookie. You will get a more tender cookie if you mix mostly by hand.

Yield: 3 dozen medium cookies

½ cup (1 stick) lightly salted butter, softened
1 cup plus 3 tablespoons packed light brown sugar
1 tablespoon nonfat dry milk powder
1 egg, lightly beaten
1 teaspoon vanilla extract
1 tablespoon water
¾ cup natural peanut butter
¼ teaspoon baking soda
1½ cups unbleached flour
1 cup roasted peanuts
6 ounces white chocolate (optional)

Preheat oven to 350° F.

The next two steps can be with electric mixer if you are rushed or the butter isn't soft enough to cream by hand.

Cream softened butter with brown sugar until well blended.

Add milk powder, egg, vanilla, and water, and mix well.

Stir in peanut butter at low speed or by hand until thoroughly incorporated.

Mix in the flour and baking soda until smooth.

Fold in roasted peanuts, chopped coarsely if you wish. If desired, stir in 6 ounces chopped white or semisweet chocolate with the peanuts.

Drop by rounded teaspoonfuls on ungreased baking sheets. If desired, press slightly flat with the tines of a fork in a crisscross pattern.

Bake at 350° for 12–15 minutes or until golden.

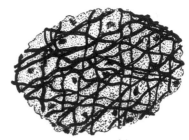

Lace Cookies

Thin, crisp, and delicate, these brown-sugary nut cookies are a most elegant accompaniment to ice cream and a fancy addition to a tray of sweets. They require a little care in removing them at just the right moment from the baking sheet, but they are definitely worth the extra effort. At Greyston Bakery we drizzle these with fine lines of bittersweet chocolate glaze, but they are also beautiful unadorned. Fancy variations are also possible: they can be rolled while hot into "cigarettes" to be filled with ganache or pastry cream, or sandwiched with bittersweet chocolate. These cookies are best when fresh and crisp. They will wilt in the heat.

Yield: 3 dozen medium cookies

6 tablespoons (¾ stick) lightly salted butter
1¼ cups brown sugar
¼ cup corn syrup
¼ cup water
1¼ cups all-purpose flour
1 cup (4 ounces) finely chopped filberts or pecans
½ teaspoon cinnamon
4 ounces bittersweet chocolate, melted, plus 1 tablespoon
*   water (optional)*

Preheat oven to 350° F.

Cream together butter and brown sugar.

Add corn syrup and water, and beat until light and smooth.

Stir in flour by hand. Mix well. Fold in chopped nuts.

Butter cookie sheets very well.

Drop batter by teaspoonfuls, allowing space for cookies to spread (about 6 cookies per 12 x 18-inch baking sheet).

Bake at 350° for 8–10 minutes. Cookies will look bubbly and just begin to brown at the edges.

Cool on the sheets for 3–4 minutes, then carefully remove with a spatula and cool on a rack. Drizzle with melted bittersweet chocolate if desired. Melt chocolate over hot water in small saucepan, and add 1 tablespoon water to thin it slightly. Drizzle in thin lines from spoon or using cake decorating tube.

Lace Cookies stay crisp at room temperature, loosely covered with plastic wrap. They do not freeze well (they get soft on thawing).

Sesame Tahini Cookies

This unusual and wholesome cookie combines both sesame seeds and tahini (sesame butter) to produce a pronounced sesame flavor, a little like that of halvah. It is especially delicious with a fresh fruit dessert. Using whole wheat pastry flour contributes to the all-natural, earthy quality, but unbleached white flour can be used if desired. These cookies can be made as drops, or the dough can be chilled for 2 hours or more and then rolled thin and cut into simple rounds. Both are delicious!

Yield: 3 dozen medium cookies

¾ cup lightly salted butter, softened
1½ cups packed light brown sugar
1 cup tahini, well mixed so that oil doesn't separate
1 egg, lightly beaten
1 teaspoon vanilla extract
1 tablespoon water
1¾ cups whole wheat pastry flour
½ teaspoon baking soda
1 cup sesame seeds

Preheat oven to 350° F.

Cream softened butter and brown sugar (an electric mixer is fine).

Add tahini and blend thoroughly.

Beat in egg, vanilla, and water until light and fluffy.

Mix in flour and baking soda by hand until blended.

Stir in sesame seeds.

Drop by rounded teaspoonfuls onto ungreased cookie sheets.

Bake for 12 minutes at 350°.

Cool on a rack, and store in an airtight container.

5 All in a Crust

TARTS AND PIES

Our tarts are baked in fluted French tart pans. The result is a simple elegance of presentation that is enhanced by the carefully prepared fillings. We make tarts in many sizes, ranging from 11 inches for restaurants to 3 inches for individual servings. Here we have reduced our recipes to make an 8-inch tart. The fluted pans with removable bottoms are readily available in gourmet cookware shops. Of course, you could bake these tarts in a regular 8-inch pie plate, but we suggest that the effect of the fluted pan is more than worth the cost of a special pan. (And incidentally, these French pans are surprisingly inexpensive.)

We offer five tarts baked in a shortbread crust. This is the same recipe we use for our shortbread cookies, so any scraps can be cut and baked to nibble on. It is a very easy dough to handle and makes a fine-textured, buttery tart crust that holds fillings well. The chapter concludes with two wonderful apple recipes, each with its own special pastry and both using flavorful Granny Smith apples.

SHORTBREAD CRUST

Yield: 1 8-inch crust

½ cup lightly salted butter at room temperature
¼ cup confectioner's sugar
½ teaspoon orange extract
1 cup sifted flour

Cream softened butter with confectioner's sugar until well blended.

Add orange extract to butter-sugar mixture and mix thoroughly.

Stir in sifted flour, mixing well. You may use your hands to work the dough thoroughly and then form it into a ball.

Chill, well wrapped with plastic wrap, for 1 hour or more.

Roll to about ⅓ inch thick on a lightly floured board.

Fit into an 8-inch fluted tart pan, trimming evenly and patching as needed.

To bake unfilled, prick several times with a fork both before baking and as soon as the crust comes from the oven. Bake for 20–25 minutes at 350°, until golden brown.

To bake filled, prebake the crust for 15 minutes, then fill and bake as directed in Pecan Tart, Pumpkin Tart, or Mince-Pecan Tart recipe.

Pecan Tart

Consistently popular with our customers, not only for its sweet, nutty goodness, but also for its excellent keeping qualities, our pecan tart seems to be everyone's favorite. Baked in a shallow French fluted pan, our tart does not have the thick, sweet filling of a conventional pecan pie, but rather is filled to the rim with lots of pecan halves nestled in a brown-sugary glaze. Try this topped with pralines 'n' cream ice cream, if you really want to gild the lily. Wrapped in a plastic bag, this tart freezes well. It can be stored at room temperature for several days, as long as it is covered.

Yield: 1 8-inch tart

1 recipe Shortbread Crust (page 92)

PECAN FILLING
¼ cup lightly salted butter
⅓ cup brown sugar
⅓ cup light corn syrup
½ teaspoon vanilla extract
1 egg
1 tablespoon flour
1½ cups pecan halves

Preheat oven to 350°.

Prepare Shortbread Crust dough in an 8-inch fluted tart pan.

Prebake crust for 15 minutes at 350° until just beginning to turn slightly golden.

Melt butter over low heat in a medium saucepan. Add brown sugar and corn syrup.

Remove from heat and allow to cool for 10 minutes.

Add vanilla, lightly beaten egg, and flour. Mix well.

Fill prepared tart shell with pecan halves, using as many nuts as it will hold.

Bake for 25–30 minutes at 350°, until evenly brown and set. Underbaking makes a softer tart. Leave it in a little longer if you like it very firm and sort of caramelized.

For a professional shiny finish, brush while warm with hot syrup made by bringing ½ cup water and ½ cup sugar to a full boil.

Cool on a rack. When completely cold, remove the rim and place tart on a plate for serving.

Fresh Fruit Tart

For a summertime delight, we line a baked Shortbread Crust with Grand Marnier Custard, arrange fresh seasonal fruits in a mosaiclike design, then brush with a clear, sparkling glaze. This tart is very perishable and fragile, is best eaten the same day, and of course should be kept well chilled. We usually use strawberries, blueberries, and sliced kiwi plus seedless red or green grapes. Occasionally we use some canned mandarin orange segments along with the fresh fruits available. It is best to avoid very juicy fruits, such as melon slices, whose juices will dilute the custard and make a delicious mess! We encourage you to be creative with the array of shapes, colors, and textures of summer's harvest.

Yield: 1 8-inch tart

1 baked Shortbread Crust (page 92)

GRAND
MARNIER
CUSTARD

¾ cup milk
¼ cup sugar
2 tablespoons flour
dash salt
2 egg yolks
1 tablespoon Grand Marnier liqueur or 1 teaspoon orange extract
½ cup (approx.) each of three kinds of fresh fruits of contrasting colors and shapes

CLEAR GLAZE *1 envelope gelatin (or kosher gel)*
1 cup cold water
½ cup sugar

Making this fruit tart is an assembly process. First each part has to be ready and cooled or chilled: the baked crust, the custard, the glaze, the sliced fruits. Both the crust and the custard can be made the day before. The actual assembly goes quickly and easily; whatever design one comes up with seems to be naturally beautiful.

Have Shortbread Crust baked and completely cool.

*To Prepare
Custard*

Heat milk to scalding (just below a boil) and remove from heat.

Combine sugar, flour, dash salt, and egg yolks in the top of a double boiler set over hot water. Stir this well; it will become light.

Gradually stir in hot milk until blended.

Cook, stirring continuously, until mixture is about to boil. Then lift it off the hot water.

Stir in the Grand Marnier liqueur or extract.

Keep stirring to help custard cool down. Then chill completely, setting the saucepan in a bath of ice water and then in the refrigerator, well covered with plastic wrap.

*To Prepare
Fruits*

Wash, dry, and slice fruits as needed. Set on paper towels to drain.

*To Prepare
Clear Glaze*

In a small saucepan, soften gelatin in cold water. Add sugar.

Heat over medium flame, stirring to dissolve both sugar and gelatin.

Chill by setting the saucepan in an ice-water bath until syrupy and slightly thickened.

*To Assemble
Tart*

Spoon custard into crust, lining it about ¾ inch deep with custard.

Arrange fruits attractively, trying to cover as much of the surface as possible, with a minimum amount of custard showing.

Spoon syrupy glaze over fruit, using just enough to give it a sparkle, but not so much that it sits in pools. If glaze gets too thick, heat it up a bit and then rechill.

Keep tart refrigerated until serving time.

Brandied Peach Tart

Originally developed as a winter alternative to our Fresh Fruit Tart, this Brandied Peach Tart is especially nice to brighten up a snowy evening. At Greyston Bakery we make a cherry tart with commercially available frozen unsweetened cherries, which we cook with tapioca and flavor with brandy. For home use, the only similar product available in the supermarket seems to be frozen unsweetened peach slices. After soaking in a brandy-flavored syrup, the sliced peaches are arranged in a fluted Shortbread Crust, then covered with a glaze. Optionally, you can decorate the tart with either cream cheese icing or swirls of fresh whipped cream.

Yield: 1 8-inch tart

1 recipe Shortbread Crust (page 92), prebaked for
15 minutes

BRANDIED   *2 cups frozen unsweetened sliced peaches*
PEACH FILLING   *½ cup water*
½ cup sugar
¼ cup plus 1 tablespoon brandy
½ cup peach preserves

TOPPING   *1 cup heavy cream whipped with ¼ cup powdered sugar*
(OPTIONAL)
or

½ recipe Cream Cheese Icing (optional; see page 115)

Have Shortbread Crust baked and completely cool.

Thaw peach slices for at least 1 hour at room temperature. They thaw fastest if you spread them out on a plate; that way you can also select 24 of the most perfect slices.

Boil together the water and sugar to form a simple syrup. Remove from heat and stir in ¼ cup brandy.

Pour syrup over selected peaches in a small, deep bowl. Turn to allow peaches to soak up flavor evenly. Let them soak for half an hour or longer.

Drain peaches well on several paper towels, patting them dry.

Carefully arrange peach slices in a slightly overlapping spiral all around the outer perimeter of the crust. Fill in the center with a spiral of the smaller pieces.

In a small saucepan, melt the peach preserves over low heat, stirring to break up any large pieces. Remove from heat and stir in 1 tablespoon brandy.

Carefully spoon on the melted preserves to form a thin glaze over the brandy-flavored peaches, giving a shiny finish. Chill.

If desired, decorate with either the Cream Cheese Icing or the whipped cream. Fill a pastry bag and using a medium star tip run a ribbon all around the tart, looping in eight places to mark each piece. Or just press eight large swirls around the outer edge, or spoon dollops of icing or whipped cream on each serving.

Refrigerate until served.

Pumpkin Tart

For an autumn specialty, we fill our fluted Shortbread Crust with a well-spiced pumpkin filling. This is excellent topped with whipped cream or ice cream for a Thanksgiving finale. Since this is essentially a custard pie, keep it under refrigeration.

Yield: 1 8-inch tart

1 recipe Shortbread Crust (page 92), prebaked for
15 minutes

PUMPKIN
FILLING

1 can (1 pound) pumpkin
½ cup sugar
½ teaspoon salt
1 teaspoon cinnamon
1 teaspoon ginger
½ teaspoon mace
½ teaspoon vanilla
¼ cup milk
3 eggs, lightly beaten

Prepare Shortbread Crust, chilling dough and rolling it to fit into an 8-inch fluted tart pan. Prebake at 350° for 15 minutes.

Preheat oven to 350° F.

Using an electric mixer, add all ingredients in the order given, beating until very creamy and smooth.

Pour into prebaked crust and spread evenly.

Bake at 350° until done, about 30–35 minutes. Cool and then store, covered with plastic wrap, in the refrigerator.

Mince-Pecan Tart

A mincemeat filling baked in a fluted Shortbread Crust, topped with pecan halves and lightly brushed with an apricot glaze, makes a distinctive holiday specialty. Our homemade mincemeat recipe, another gift to us from the Tassajara Bakery, is very easy to make and has a wonderful tangy and spicy flavor. Although this recipe is firmly rooted in the English tradition, our version has no meat in it and, in fact, for those whose families came from Eastern Europe the filling is reminiscent of a thick brandied fruit compote. If you have mincemeat or compote fans at your house, try this delicious rendition of an old favorite. We also use this tasty mincemeat in our turnovers during the holidays (see page 69).

Yield: 1 8-inch tart

1 recipe Shortbread Crust (page 92)

MINCEMEAT
FILLING

4 unpeeled tart apples, chopped into ½–1-inch dice
juice and rind of 1 orange
juice and rind of 1 lemon
¾ cup brown sugar
½ cup dark raisins
½ cup golden raisins
½ cup chopped dates
½ teaspoon salt
½ teaspoon cinnamon
½ teaspoon nutmeg
½ teaspoon ground cloves
1 teaspoon vanilla
2 tablespoons brandy or rum (or to taste)
½ cup chopped pecans
8 large pecan halves

GLAZE

3 tablespoons apricot preserves
3 tablespoons water

Prepare Shortbread Crust, chilling dough and rolling it ⅓ inch thick to fit an 8-inch fluted tart pan.

Preheat oven to 350° F.

Underbake the crust—keep it in the oven for only 15 minutes. Prick any bubbles. Let cool while you prepare filling. Do not turn oven off.

Mix together all filling ingredients except brandy or rum in a heavy saucepan and simmer together, covered, for 25–35 minutes over low heat.

Uncover and let filling boil gently to evaporate extra juice, until it is nice and thick. Take care because it can easily burn at this stage.

Stir in brandy or rum to taste.

Stir in chopped pecans.

Spoon into prebaked crust and smooth evenly.

Bake for about 30–35 minutes.

Let cool. Then place 8 pecan halves evenly around tart, about 1 inch in from the outer edge.

Over low heat, heat apricot preserves with water, mixing well. Spoon or brush glaze carefully over pecan-topped tart.

Refrigerate covered. Let tart come to room temperature or warm it slightly for serving.

TWO WITH APPLES

French Apple Tart

Baked in a special tangy crust, this tart is filled with overlapping slices of Granny Smith apples brushed with a lemony cinnamon glaze. Despite its elegant "patisserie" appearance, it is very easily made in the home kitchen—not even a rolling pin is required! The apples are baked "naked" right in the crust, then the cinnamon glaze is brushed on while the tart is still very warm from the oven.

Yield: 1 8-inch tart

CRUST	*2¼ cups flour* *¼ cup sugar* *1 cup sweet butter at room temperature* *2 tablespoons cider vinegar* *2 tablespoons water*
APPLE FILLING	*3 large Granny Smith apples* *1 tablespoon flour mixed with 4 tablespoons sugar*
LEMON- CINNAMON GLAZE	*4 teaspoons cornstarch* *½ cup water* *½ cup sugar* *2 tablespoons lemon juice* *1 teaspoon cinnamon*

Crust   Mix together the flour and sugar.

Cut in the softened butter with a fork or pastry blender, incorporating it evenly.

Mix together the vinegar and water in a measuring cup (should total ¼ cup). Sprinkle this liquid mixture over the butter and flour, stirring well until a soft dough is formed.

Press dough into an 8-inch fluted tart pan with your hands, making it as even as possible on all sides.

Preheat oven to 350° F.

Apple Filling   Peel and thinly slice 3 apples.

Arrange apples over crust, slightly overlapping the slices as you work around the outside circle. Similarly, form an inner circle of overlapping slices.

Repeat, forming two layers of thin-sliced apples in a circular pattern.

Mix together 1 tablespoon flour with 4 tablespoons sugar, and sprinkle this over the top layer of apples.

Bake at 350° for about 25–30 minutes. Apples should be tender and slightly brown at the edges.

Lemon-
Cinnamon
Glaze   Mix cornstarch with cold water; then add sugar, lemon juice, and cinnamon.

Heat over medium flame, stirring constantly until thickened. Remove from heat.

Brush warm glaze onto warm tart, giving it an even, shiny brown topping.

Let cool before serving.

Should there be any leftovers, refrigerate overnight.

Deep-Dish Apple Pie

Simply old-fashioned and wonderful, our apple pie features an all-butter crust over a heaping mound of cinnamon-dusted Granny Smith apples. Everyone likes it warm from the oven, just as is or garnished with ice cream or sharp Cheddar.

CRUST
2¼ cups flour
1 cup lightly salted butter
4–6 tablespoons ice water
egg wash: 1 egg beaten with 2 tablespoons water and
*   1 teaspoon sugar*

FILLING
6–7 Granny Smith apples
½ cup light brown sugar
2 tablespoons instant tapioca
1 teaspoon cinnamon

SYRUP
¼ cup juice from apples
⅛ cup brown sugar
1 teaspoon cornstarch
1 tablespoon lemon juice
1 teaspoon cinnamon

Our production procedure involves tossing the apples with sugar and letting them stand for at least 1 hour, then pressing out all the liquid. This juice is later made into a syrup, which is poured into the pie through a hole in the top crust after it is baked. This is done to prevent excessive shrinking of the apples during baking, thus minimizing any large gaps under the crust or the caved-in look that comes from shrinking cooked apples. The details of this procedure are as follows.

Peel and slice 6–7 apples, toss with brown sugar, and let sit for 1 hour or longer while you make the crust.

Cut butter into flour with pastry blender or fork until crumbly. Add the ice water by spoonfuls until the dough can be

Fresh Fruit Tart

Pecan Tarts and French Apple Tarts

formed into a loose ball. (If you add enough water to keep all the dough fragments tightly together in a ball, the crust will be pasty instead of flaky.) Cover with plastic wrap and chill for about a half-hour.

Divide dough in half. Roll out to fit into an 8-inch pie pan. Trim neatly, patching any holes.

Drain and save the juice that has come from the apple-sugar mixture. Press apples with your hands to get as much liquid out as possible. Toss apples with cinnamon and tapioca. Fill pastry-lined pie pan with apples. They should be mounded up in a high, rounded heap. Preheat oven to 400° F.

Roll dough for top crust on waxed paper. Lifting the paper, turn pastry over onto the apple-filled pie. Trim edges evenly with a knife or scissors. Flute edges together with a fork or between thumb and forefinger.

Cut a star-shaped opening about 1 inch in diameter in the center of the top crust, using a small cookie cutter or a sharp knife. Brush lightly with egg wash.

Turn oven down to 350° as soon as you put the pie in.

Bake for 50–60 minutes at 350°.

Meanwhile, prepare syrup. Mix together ¼ cup of the saved apple juice, cornstarch, brown sugar, lemon juice, and cinnamon in a small saucepan.

· Bring to a boil and stir until thick. Remove from heat. Keep warm.

When the pie is done, carefully pour the warm syrup into the hole in the top crust. Let cool for at least half an hour before serving.

Alternative method for the home baker in a hurry: Toss apple slices as above, adding all the syrup ingredients except the apple juice. All other directions remain the same, but of course you eliminate the step of pouring syrup into the hole after the pie is baked.

6

Happy Endings

IRRESISTIBLE CAKES

It has been constantly amazing how delicious and beautiful these cakes have turned out in our home test kitchens. We have given rather detailed directions for mixing procedures and finishing (frosting and decorating), sharing with you the techniques of our professional finishers quite directly. Please read over each recipe completely before you begin. In some cases there are several steps that should be fully understood before you are up to your elbows in chocolate. The recipe for the icing or topping and finishing instructions are included with each cake recipe. We wish you many happy endings, hoping that this will be just a beginning in your discovery of what good things can be made "from scratch" in your own kitchen.

GREYSTON SPECIALTY CAKES

Queen of Sheba Torte

This dense, rich chocolate almond torte is closely related to the famous French Reine de Saba and the Austrian Sacher torte. Despite its elegant origins, it is fairly simple to complete with a "professional" touch in the home kitchen. This recipe can be made a day ahead but should be removed from the refrigerator several hours before serving. The cake can be frozen as well, but be sure to wrap it airtight in a plastic bag. This recipe can be easily doubled if you need to serve 16. We have made it as a two-layer torte but have found that because it is so rich and dense, most customers prefer the single layer. One lovely variation that follows is the Queen of Sheba Petit Four—exquisite almond-studded, chocolate-covered rectangles perfect for an elegant dessert tray. Beautifully shaped petits fours can also be made with a sharp metal cookie cutter. We have made them heart-shaped topped with a pink rosebud for Valentine's Day as well as in the shape of shamrocks for Saint Patrick's Day. The round 8-inch cake layer can also be cut with a paper pattern into a heart shape, then glazed and decorated with "I love you" in chocolate.

Yield: 1 8-inch cake

CAKE	*4 ounces semisweet baking chocolate*
	¼ cup finely ground unblanched almonds
	½ cup lightly salted butter
	2 eggs
	¼ cup flour
	¼ cup sugar
	¼ teaspoon baking soda
GLAZE	*2 tablespoons apricot jam or preserves*
	8 whole unblanched almonds
	4 ounces semisweet chocolate
	3 ounces sweet butter

Melt semisweet chocolate over hot water. Remove from heat when melted. Grind whole unblanched almonds in an electric blender or food mill. Set aside.

Preheat oven to 350° F.

Cream butter and sugar with electric mixer until soft and uniform. Beat in eggs until mixture is light and fluffy. Stir in melted chocolate. Mix well until thick.

Fold in flour, soda, and ground almonds by hand.

Pour into an 8-inch round cake pan that has been buttered and lightly floured.

Bake at 350° for 25 minutes or until cake begins to shrink from sides of pan and center springs back when touched gently.

Cool completely before glazing (this is important, otherwise the glaze will run off the warm cake).

To Glaze and Decorate

Melt 2 tablespoons apricot jam over very low heat in a small saucepan. Stir in 8–10 whole almonds, stirring until well coated with melted jam.

Separately place each coated almond on a plate. Let them cool and set.

Melt semisweet chocolate and *sweet* butter together over low heat. Stir briskly with a wire whisk or fork to blend butter and chocolate.

Remove from heat and let cool 3–4 minutes.

To Finish the Torte

This is a poured glaze, not a spread frosting. You will be pouring the glaze twice, with the cake taking a short trip to the refrigerator in between. You will need a cooling rack of some sort as well as the willingness to become chocolaty yourself!

Place the cake layer on a rack. Tilt it slightly and spoon the glaze onto the sides, using a knife to even it out.

Set the rack on a cookie sheet to catch the drips, and then spoon the warm glaze in a thin, even layer over the top, again using a knife to distribute it evenly if necessary.

Chill the cake in the refrigerator for about 10 minutes.

Warm the glaze over the hot water, and keep the heat low while the cake is chilling.

Pour the final layer of glaze, beginning with the sides, using a spatula or knife to even it on the sides. Then pour all of the remaining glaze evenly over the top. You will not want to have any visible knife streaks, so don't go back and spread once the glaze has started to set.

Chill again on the rack in the refrigerator for 10 minutes.

Decorate with the 8 glazed almonds by placing them, pointed end toward the center, 1 inch in from the outer edge—first marking one-half, then one-quarter, and finally one-eighth of the cake. Each serving will thus have one glazed almond marking its center.

Variations

1. For Passover, substitute margarine for butter and matzo cake meal for flour. Use the Chocolate Water Glaze listed in the Chocolate Mousse Cake recipe (page 135).

2. For those who love the marriage of oranges and chocolate: Add 1 tablespoon grated orange rind to batter. Decorate cake with glazed mandarin oranges or candied orange slices or peel.

3. Prepare a paper pattern for an 8-inch heart, and use it to cut the baked cake layer (it cuts easily if semifrozen). Pour on glaze following directions above. Decorate or write your message with butter cream (chocolate or vanilla or your choice of color or flavor added) pressed through a pastry bag with a small tip. You might want to practice writing on a piece of cardboard. It just takes a while to master the combination of squeezing pressure and writing speed. These Queen of Sheba Hearts make wonderful homemade valentines or Mother's Day gifts.

Queen of Sheba Petit Four

Please read all directions for mixing and preparing and finishing given above. The only thing different here is the shape and size.

Double recipe for cake and bittersweet glaze given above.

This recipe makes 25 petits fours, so glaze 25 almonds, using 4 tablespoons preserves for the glaze.

Bake in 13 x 9 x 2-inch pan for about 30 minutes, or until cake starts to pull away from sides of pan.

Cool 5 minutes in the pan, then turn upside down onto large board to cool completely. Prepare apricot-glazed almonds.

Prepare bittersweet glaze, keeping warm over hot water.

Cut cake lengthwise into five 1½-inch strips, then crosswise into five even rectangles, each about 2¼ inches long, *or* cut into hearts or other simple shapes with a sharp metal cookie cutter.

Place a cake rack over a cookie sheet to catch drips.

Spear one piece from the top (actually the bottom when it was baking) and hold it over the pan with glaze, spooning the glaze on the sides while turning the fork. Then place on rack and spoon glaze over the top. Repeat for all 36 pieces. Let chill, or at least set in a cool place, for 20 minutes. Then repour the top, also using a knife to spread glaze on the sides. Glaze should be smooth and very even. Chill.

Decorate with one glazed almond in the center of each.

Yield: 25 petits fours.

Sour Cream Poppy Seed Cake

Delicate white sour cream cake dotted with an abundance of poppy seeds, topped with a rich cream cheese icing—this is perhaps our most distinctive cake. With origins in Hungarian cuisine, and good recipe ideas from the Tassajara Bakery, our basic poppy seed cake has proven very versatile. We make a plain uniced ring called the Poppy Seed Pound Cake, an iced Poppy Seed Sheet Cake that serves twelve, a three-layer Carousel for a fancy dessert, and a wedding cake. The cake itself is very easy to make. We recommend the use of an electric mixer. The only tricky part is in working with the cream cheese icing without the benefit of professional finishing tools or training. This cake is best fresh; once it is iced, it must be refrigerated so that the icing doesn't spoil. Remove it from the refrigerator an hour before serving so that it can come up to room temperature. The refrigerator tends to dry the cake out, so we recommend that you assemble it the day you will be serving it. You can bake the layers the day before and wrap them well in plastic wrap when cool.

Yield: 2 8-inch layers or
1 13 x 9-inch sheet
or 1 8-inch ring

1 cup butter at room temperature
1⅓ cups sugar
6 eggs, separated
2 teaspoons vanilla
2 cups flour
1½ teaspoons baking soda
½ teaspoon salt
1 cup sour cream
½ cup poppy seeds

CREAM CHEESE
ICING

8 ounces cream cheese (not whipped) at room temperature
4 ounces sweet butter at room temperature
2 cups powdered sugar, sifted

Preheat oven to 350° F.

Prepare desired pan(s)—two 8-inch layer pans or a 13 x 9 x 2-inch sheet pan or an 8-inch ring pan—by buttering well and dusting lightly with flour.

Cream butter and sugar.

Beat in egg yolks thoroughly. Add vanilla.

Sift together flour, baking soda, and salt in a small bowl.

Alternately add dry ingredients and sour cream to the butter mixture, mixing well after each addition. Keep mixing until very smooth.

Stir in poppy seeds until evenly distributed.

By hand, using a spatula, fold in stiffly beaten egg whites, carefully incorporating them into the batter.

Pour into prepared pan(s).

Bake at 350° for 25–30 minutes for layers, 35–40 minutes for sheet, 50–55 minutes for ring. Watch carefully. Cake should pull from sides of pan, and a toothpick should come out clean from the center.

Cool for 5 minutes in pan, then turn and release onto rack, cooling completely before finishing.

To Ice and Decorate

Soften butter and cream cheese at room temperature for a few hours.

Beat cream cheese and butter together with an electric mixer until they are completely incorporated and the mixture is very light and creamy.

Mix in sifted powdered sugar, 1 cup at a time, beating well after each addition.

Chill icing in a bowl covered with plastic wrap for about 1 hour before spreading.

Prepare cake layers before frosting as directed for your variation.

Poppy Seed Carousel or Layer Cake

In our bakery we use an unfluted ring for the Carousel, cut into three layers horizontally. We do not ice the sides of the Carousel. For the layer cake, you can cut each layer in half horizontally. Place carefully on waxed paper. You can also leave this as a two-layer cake.

Place bottom layer cut side down on cake plate covered with paper doily if desired.

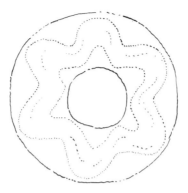

Spoon a ribbon of icing in a zigzag pattern on layer, spreading slightly with a spatula dipped in hot water.

Place next layer on top, pressing down gently to even and to help layers stick together.

Repeat frosting and layering, making sure that top layer is placed cut side down.

Spread icing on top very smoothly and evenly, dipping knife or spatula in very hot water constantly.

Trim excess frosting from sides and (if using ring) from hole in center using a soup spoon dipped in very hot water.

Chill cake for 10–20 minutes.

Decorate with eight swirls of chilled icing squeezed through a pastry bag with a star tip, as in the illustration.

If you like more cake and less frosting, splitting the cake in two gives a more satisfying cake-to-frosting balance. However, the three-layer cake is more eye-catching.

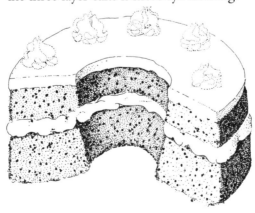

*Poppyseed
Sheet Cake*

Place cake on board, tray, or large, heavy cardboard covered with paper doilies.

Trim about ¼ inch on all sides, thus removing the edges where the batter touched the pan, and leaving a cut surface on the sides. This cake will be iced on the top only, and the cut sides are quite lovely showing off all the poppy seed dots.

Spread chilled icing on top of cake quite thickly with a bowl knife or spatula dipped in very hot water, making sure the icing overhangs the entire edge. It should be smooth and very even.

Trim the excess icing with knife dipped in hot water as needed.

Chill entire cake for about 20 minutes.

Cut into 12 even squares with a serrated knife: do not separate pieces; keep cake whole but scored. (This is optional; you might prefer to leave it uncut.)

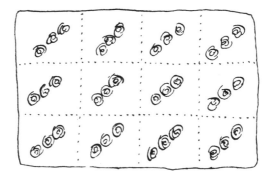

Decorate with swirls of chilled icing pressed through a pastry bag with a star tip according to the illustration.

As a variation, you might prefer to ice the sides as in the usual sheet cake. That way the cake will stay fresh longer. You should increase the cream cheese frosting recipe by one-half: 12 ounces cream cheese, 6 ounces sweet butter, 3 cups powdered sugar.

*Poppy Seed
Pound Cake*

Dust the cooled ring with powdered sugar rubbed through a sieve with the back of a spoon.

For a beautiful lacy design, we often place a doily over the cake, sift powdered sugar over that, and carefully remove the doily with two hands, leaving a stenciled pattern.

This recipe can be divided in half and baked in an 8-inch loaf pan for a smaller cake.

The Grand Duchess

Our most sophisticated dessert cake, the subtly orange-flavored Grand Duchess is enriched with diced filberts, soaked in Grand Marnier liqueur, and then layered with orange marmalade and covered with our bittersweet chocolate glaze. Most likely to appeal to the adults in your family, this cake makes a spectacular grand finale for the most elegant dinner. Because of the moistness provided by the liqueur, it keeps very well for several days if cut edges are covered with plastic wrap. No refrigeration is needed, except in warm, humid weather. The Grand Duchess is most flavorful when served at room temperature.

Yield: 1 8-inch layer cake

⅔ cup finely diced filberts or pecans or walnuts
¾ cup butter at room temperature
1 cup sugar
3 eggs
1 tablespoon orange extract or grated orange peel
1½ cups flour
1½ teaspoons baking soda
½ cup sour cream
¼ cup Grand Marnier liqueur
1 cup orange marmalade

GLAZE   *4 ounces semisweet chocolate*
3 ounces sweet butter

Preheat oven to 350° F.
Prepare two 8-inch cake pans by generously buttering, then lightly flouring.

Top with the fourth layer. Use no marmalade on this one.

Spread the sides and top with the chocolate glaze, using a knife or spatula. Chill cake for 10 minutes, keeping glaze warm over hot water.

Pour remaining glaze over top, working quickly so that a smooth surface is formed.

Dust the top with 2 tablespoons ground nuts, evenly distributed.

Variation

If you don't want to use liqueur, substitute ¼ cup orange-flavored simple syrup made by boiling together ½ cup water and ½ cup powdered sugar for 10 minutes, then adding 1 teaspoon orange extract. This will moisten the cake without alcohol. This syrup could also be used half and half with the liqueur if you don't want a heavy Grand Marnier taste.

Chop nuts on a wooden board to a small (⅛–¼-inch) dice. Finely grind 2 tablespoons of the diced nuts in a blender for the topping, and set aside.

Cream butter and sugar until very light and creamy.

Add eggs, beating well.

Stir in orange extract or peel.

Sift together flour and baking soda.

Alternately add flour mixture and sour cream to butter mixture, mixing well after each addition.

By hand, fold in the ½ cup diced nuts, mixing until well blended.

Pour into prepared pans, distributing evenly.

Bake for about 30 minutes or until edges pull from sides of pan and a toothpick inserted in the center comes out clean.

Cool for 5 minutes in pan, then turn onto cake rack to finish cooling.

To Finish

Melt semisweet chocolate and sweet butter over hot water in top of double boiler.

Split cooled layers in half horizontally with a serrated knife.

Brush liqueur on cut surface of layers, repeating until it has all been absorbed.

Place first layer on plate, top side down. Spread with ⅓ cup orange marmalade.

Repeat the marmalade for the next two layers.

Classic Carrot Cake

Our moist carrot cake is spiced with cinnamon and fresh lemon rind, studded with raisins and walnuts, and frosted with cream cheese icing.

Yield: 1 8-inch layer cake

2 cups light brown sugar
½ cup soy oil
½ cup buttermilk
¼ cup honey
3 eggs
2 cups flour
1½ teaspoons cinnamon
½ teaspoon salt
1 teaspoon baking soda
1 teaspoon grated lemon rind
2 cups finely grated carrots
½ cup raisins
½ cup chopped walnuts

CREAM CHEESE
ICING

8 ounces cream cheese at room temperature
4 ounces sweet butter at room temperature
2 cups powdered sugar
1 cup finely chopped walnuts

Preheat oven to 350° F.

Butter and lightly flour two 8-inch cake pans.

Mix together sugar, oil, buttermilk, honey, and eggs in the large bowl of a mixer. Beat until light.

Sift together flour, cinnamon, salt, and baking soda. Add this gradually to the egg mixture. Stir in lemon rind, grated carrots, raisins, and chopped walnuts. (You can coarsely chop the nuts if you like a chunky quality, or finely chop them for a more even texture.)

Pour into prepared pans, distributing evenly.

Bake at 350° for 30–35 minutes. The sides should begin to pull away, and the center will spring back when lightly pressed.

Turn onto a rack and cool completely. While cake is cooling, prepare frosting. It needs to chill 1 hour before using.

Cream Cheese Icing

Beat together the softened cream cheese and butter with an electric mixer until very creamy. Gradually beat in sugar. Chill for about 1 hour before using.

Frost between layers and on top and sides with Cream Cheese Icing. We "comb" the top and sides of our cake with a special decorator's tool available at gourmet cookware shops (see drawing on page 131). Lacking that, you might just swirl the top frosting attractively with a spatula or butter knife.

Press chopped walnuts generously into the frosted sides.

Nana's Fruit Cake

Filled with fruits and nuts, our brandy-soaked fruit cakes are based on a traditional recipe from the grandmother of one of our bakers. We offer two versions here, both identical in mixing and baking procedures: a traditional cake using glacé fruits, citron, and cherries and an all-natural version in which natural dried fruits (with no coloring or preservatives) and nuts are used exclusively. Both are chewy, dark, and flavorful. They are best made at least one week before serving. We include vegetable oil for moistness and a reduction in the crumbliness of the cake. Always slice a fruit cake when it is cold from the refrigerator to avoid breakage.

Yield: 2 rings or 8 x 4-inch loaves

BASIC FRUIT CAKE BATTER

¾ cup lightly salted butter
1½ cups light brown sugar
3 eggs, lightly beaten
¼ cup oil
1½ cups flour, sifted
½ teaspoon ground cinnamon
¼ teaspoon ground mace
¼ teaspoon ground nutmeg
¼ teaspoon ground cloves
¼ cup apple juice
2–4 ounces brandy (poured on after baking)

TRADITIONAL CANDIED FRUIT

1 cup raisins
1 cup currants
8 ounces dates, chopped
7–8 ounces diced citron
16 ounces diced glacé fruits

8 ounces glacé cherries, halved
1 cup whole almonds
1 cup chopped walnuts
¼ cup cooled coffee

or

ALL-NATURAL
FRUIT

1 cup dark raisins
1 cup golden raisins
1 cup currants
8 ounces dates, chopped
1 cup chopped dried apricots
1 cup chopped dried pineapple
1 cup whole almonds
1 cup chopped walnuts
¼ cup apple juice

Preheat oven to 280° F.

To prepare loaf or ring pans (one of each, or two 8 x 4-inch loaves), butter the pan, then cut a strip of brown paper the width of the pan to line the bottom and two sides, and butter the paper too. For a ring pan, trace a circle on brown paper and line the bottom only.

Soak the raisins and currants in boiling water to cover; drain before using.

Cream butter with brown sugar until smooth.

Add lightly beaten eggs and oil. Mix well.

Sift in flour and spices, stirring.

Add apple juice and drained fruits.

Add coffee or additional apple juice and the nuts.

Mix very well, coating everything evenly with batter.

Divide into prepared pans, smoothing top with spatula.

Bake at 280° for 1 hour and 45 minutes, or up to 2 hours, depending on size of pan. Test for doneness with a toothpick in the center.

Leave in pan to cool.

Pour 1–2 ounces brandy over each cake in pan. Let soak overnight.

The next day, remove cakes from pans and wrap tightly in plastic wrap. Store in a cool place.

Casablanca Cake

Our Casablanca is a simple sour cream pound cake intriguingly spiced with car-damom. We bake it in both 8- and 10-inch bundt pans, and over the years have offered various finishing touches: sifted powdered sugar, bittersweet chocolate glaze, orange icing, and mandarin orange and chocolate. We have also glazed the ring with a pecan and caramel topping that was fantastic. Most of our customers have continued to request the Casablanca with the plain powdered sugar; this allows the subtle cardamom flavor to be appreciated most fully and makes the cake an excellent dessert accompaniment to fresh fruit compote or sorbet, and a perfect pound cake for Sunday afternoon coffee.

Yield: 1 10-inch ring

1 cup butter at room temperature
1½ cups sugar
3 eggs
2 cups flour, sifted
1½ teaspoons ground cardamom
¼ teaspoon salt
2 teaspoons baking soda
1 cup sour cream

Preheat oven to 325° F.

Butter and flour a 10-inch bundt pan.

Cream butter and sugar well. (An electric mixer is recommended.) Beat in eggs thoroughly.

Sift together flour, cardamom, salt, and baking soda, into a separate bowl. Alternately add the flour mixture and the sour cream to the butter mixture in the mixer bowl, beating well after each addition until batter is very smooth.

Pour batter into prepared pan, distributing evenly with a rubber spatula. Bake at 325° for about 45 – 50 minutes or until cake pulls away from sides of pan and toothpick comes out clean from center.

Queen of Sheba Petit Fours and Queen of Sheba Torte

Sour Cream Poppy Seed Cake

Cool in pan on rack for about 5 minutes, then turn over and release onto rack to finish cooling.

To Finish   When the cake is completely cooled, choose *one* of the following:

1. Dust cake with powdered sugar rubbed through a sieve.

2. Drizzle with bittersweet glaze made from 3 ounces semisweet chocolate and 2 ounces (4 tablespoons) sweet butter melted over hot water. Spoon over top, letting glaze run down the grooves.

3. Drizzle with orange icing made from ¾ cup sifted powdered sugar, 2 tablespoons orange juice, and 1 teaspoon grated orange rind (fresh or dried). Spoon over the top, letting glaze drip down the sides.

4. Decorate glazed cake with 8 or 10 mandarin orange segments placed on the larger fluted grooves around the crown of the cake. If desired, pour 2 tablespoons reserved glaze over the center of the orange segments.

5. Make Pecan Caramel Glaze as follows.

PECAN CARAMEL   *1 cup pecan halves*
GLAZE   *2 cups sugar*
                 ½ cup water
                 1 teaspoon lemon juice
                 1½ cups heavy cream

First, crown the cooled cake with pecans. Place as many pecan halves as you can manage on the top in a pleasing jumble.

Prepare caramel syrup by boiling together the sugar, water, and lemon juice in a heavy, deep saucepan over medium heat until it turns golden. Watch this carefully and stir constantly. It may seem to crystallize; just keep stirring until it turns color and melts down. At the same time heat the heavy cream in another pot on a low flame until just below boiling. At the point when the syrup is caramelizing, take it off the stove and slowly and carefully pour the hot cream into the syrup, stirring it in. Be careful; it may sputter at the beginning. It is useful to have someone else pour the cream while you stir. The mixture will quickly turn into caramel "sauce."

Pour the caramel glaze all over the cake and its pecan crown, encouraging graceful drips down the sides. Any leftover caramel is delicious on ice cream.

Chocolate Spice Bundt Cake

A wonderful variation of the Casablanca, this chocolate cardamom cake with a rich chocolate ganache glaze has been a Christmas specialty item. We think you will appreciate both the fascinating blend of spice and chocolate and the ease with which the cake can be made. It keeps well at room temperature, but cut surfaces should be covered with plastic wrap.

Yield: 1 10-inch ring

1 cup butter
1½ cups sugar
4 eggs
6 ounces semisweet chocolate, melted
2 cups flour, sifted
1½ teaspoons ground cardamom
¼ teaspoon salt
2 teaspoons baking soda
1 cup sour cream

CHOCOLATE GANACHE GLAZE

1 cup heavy cream
6 ounces semisweet chocolate

Preheat oven to 325° F.

Melt semisweet chocolate over hot water in top of double boiler.

Butter (do not flour) a 10-inch bundt pan.

Cream butter and sugar well. (An electric mixer is recommended.)

Beat in eggs thoroughly.

Add melted chocolate and mix well.

Sift together the flour, cardamom, salt, and soda into a separate bowl.

Alternately add the flour mixture and the sour cream to the chocolate mixture in the mixer bowl, beating well after each addition until batter is very smooth.

Pour batter into prepared pan, distributing evenly with a rubber spatula.

Bake at 325° for 45–50 minutes or until cake pulls away from sides of pan and a toothpick comes out clean from the center.

Cool in pan on rack for 5 minutes, then turn over and release onto rack to finish cooling.

Ganache Glaze

Heat cream in heavy saucepan until it is just below a boil.

Add the chocolate and stir constantly with a wooden spoon until it is totally melted and completely merged with the cream.

Cool until very warm, but not hot, and pour over cooled cake generously, letting it drip attractively down the sides. If you cover the cake completely with glaze, it will stay moist longer.

This glaze thickens as it gets cold. If you want it to set quickly, refrigerate for 30 minutes.

To use this Chocolate Ganache Glaze as a Ganache Filling, just prepare this recipe and chill until very thick. Use sandwiched between cookies or as a cake filling.

CHEESE CAKES

In response to our customers' wishes we finally developed a rich New York cheese cake for our bakery line. Our original hesitation was only that there were already so many wonderful cheese cakes available in New York. After lots of experimentation we came up with two distinct types: an Italian-style ricotta cheese cake and a classic cream cheese version. For the most part we are selling the cream cheese version, which we offer plain or with fresh berries in season. Cheesecakes are very easy to make, but are much easier with an 8- or 10-inch spring-form pan with a removable bottom. If you bake the cheese cake in a regular cake pan, you can follow the instructions given at the end of the Cream Cheese Cake recipe for easy removal from the pan.

Cream Cheese Cake

Yield: 1 8-inch cake. Double recipe for a 10-inch pan.

1½ pounds cream cheese at room temperature
1 cup sugar
2 eggs, lightly beaten
1 teaspoon vanilla extract
¾ cup sour cream
4 tablespoons flour
1 teaspoon freshly grated lemon rind

Prepare 8- or 8½-inch spring-form pan or cake pan by buttering generously.

Preheat oven to 350° F.

Place large roasting pan of hot water on bottom rack of oven.

Cream the softened cream cheese with a wooden spoon until smooth and soft, or use an electric mixer.

Add sugar, mixing well.

Stir in eggs, vanilla, sour cream, flour, and lemon rind, and mix until very smooth and creamy (an electric mixer on low speed is OK, but do not beat at high speed or for a long time).

Pour batter into prepared pan, spreading evenly.

Bake at 350° on top rack over the hot-water pan for 35–45 minutes for the 8-inch cake. The center will be set and the sides just beginning to pull away from the pan. The 10-inch size will take at least 1 hour to bake.

Turn off oven, open door, and leave cake sitting there for about 20 minutes. Set on cake rack to finish cooling.

When cool, remove sides of spring-form pan. Chill in refrigerator for several hours before serving.

With regular cake pan, chill cake overnight in pan. The next day, briefly warm bottom of pan over a stove burner. Then turn it over onto a plate covered with plastic wrap. Flip it over right side up using another plate, and the plastic should just peel off without any damage to the surface. Voilà! For a finishing touch, try the following recipe.

FRESH BERRY
TOPPING

1 pint fresh berries in season, washed and very dry
1 envelope unflavored gelatin
½ cup sugar
1 cup water

Soften gelatin in cold water in small saucepan.

Cook over low heat, adding sugar and stirring constantly until both gelatin and sugar are dissolved. This mixture will become clear and be just beginning to boil. Remove from heat.

Cool gelatin mixture, setting pan in a bath of ice cubes and cold water, until it becomes syrupy but will still pour off a spoon.

While gelatin is cooling, arrange washed and well-drained fruits on top of chilled cheese cake in a pleasing pattern.

Pour gelatin mix over fruit with a spoon, forming a clear and sparkling glaze. If your gelatin mixture gets too thick, just heat it up for a short while and start again.

Store under refrigeration at all times—this is a perishable cake.

Ricotta Cheese Cake

This Italian specialty has an interesting texture and is really quite a nutritious, high-protein dessert. Ricotta Cheese Cake should always be chilled for several hours or overnight before serving. It is easily made but does require an extra few hours to press the cheese. Don't skip or hurry this step, or you will get a somewhat watery cake.

Yield: 1 8-inch cake. Double
recipe for a 10-inch pan.

2 pounds ricotta cheese, pressed and drained for 2 hours
4 eggs
4 tablespoons flour
1 cup sugar
1 teaspoon grated lemon rind
1 teaspoon lemon juice
1 teaspoon vanilla extract

To press ricotta, place it in a cheesecloth-lined colander or strainer, put a plate on top of the cheese, and weight it down with a heavy jar or can. Let it drain over a bowl for about 2 hours.

Preheat oven to 400° F. (It will be turned down when cake goes in.)

Place large roasting pan of hot water on bottom rack of oven.

Butter an 8- or 9-inch spring-form pan.

Beat eggs into ricotta one at a time until very smooth.

Add flour and sugar, mixing well.

Stir in lemon rind, lemon juice, and vanilla.

Pour into buttered spring-form pan and spread evenly.

Turn oven down to 350°.

Bake on top rack over pan of water for 1 hour and 10 minutes or until set.

Turn off the heat, open the oven door, and leave cake inside for 30 minutes.

Let cool and then remove rim and refrigerate overnight.

Cover with fresh fruit topping if desired (see recipe listed with Cream Cheese Cake, page 123).

7 Elegant Expansions on the Basics

CHIFFON LAYER CAKES

Airy, light, and delicate, these cakes are baked in two 8-inch rounds, then split in half to be lavishly layered with whipped cream or butter cream fillings. These chiffon cakes require an electric mixer to get the egg whites standing tall, and a gentle hand folding in the other ingredients. We recommend that the whipped cream and mousse cakes be assembled the day you wish to serve them. The layers can be baked the day before and covered with plastic wrap when cool. All the mousse cakes can also be made in advance and frozen. Please don't let the elaborate finishing directions intimidate you—these cakes are delicious even without the swirls and shavings. We just wanted you to have directions from our professional finishing room should you feel inspired to present something that looks as spectacular as it tastes.

YELLOW CHIFFON LAYERS

Yield: 1 8-inch layer cake

6 egg whites
1½ cups sugar
4 egg yolks
½ cup vegetable oil
½ cup water
1 teaspoon vanilla
1½ cups flour
3 teaspoons baking powder
dash salt

Preheat oven to 350° F.

Generously butter two round 8-inch cake pans.

You will need three bowls (two large, one small).

Beat egg whites until soft peaks form. Gradually add ½ cup sugar while continuing to beat until very stiff in large bowl of mixer.

Mix egg yolks, oil, water, and vanilla together in a small bowl.

Sift together the dry ingredients into the other large bowl— 1 cup sugar, flour, baking powder, and salt.

Add the egg yolk mixture to the dry ingredients. Mix well.

Fold in stiffly beaten egg whites and gently incorporate.

Pour into prepared pans.

Bake at 350° for about 25 minutes, until sides shrink and top springs back in the center.

Turn onto a rack immediately and let cool.

Winter Damask Cake

This white-on-white creation is made with our yellow chiffon cake triple-layered with White Chocolate Rum Mousse, covered with a white chocolate glaze, and finished with sliced almonds. Technically, according to the legal description of foods, "white chocolate" is not chocolate but rather a blend of ingredients, primarily cocoa butter, sugar, and vanilla. By whatever name, this is a most unusual and beautiful dessert. Tom, our computer programmer, called it "the ultimate Twinkie!" Certainly in a class by itself, this cake is the delectable and elegant answer for those who dissent from the majority passion for chocolate.

For this recipe, we tested using Tobler Narcisse bars of white chocolate, available in good markets. All together we needed four 6-ounce bars, or 1½ pounds if you buy white chocolate at a candy store.

1 recipe Yellow Chiffon Layers (page 126), baked and cooled
¼ cup rum to brush on layers
2 ounces sliced almonds for finishing

WHITE CHOCOLATE RUM MOUSSE	
	¼ cup sugar
	4 tablespoons dark rum
	4 ounces white chocolate
	2 tablespoons heavy cream
	2 egg whites, stiffly beaten
	1–2 cups heavy cream, whipped

WHITE CHOCOLATE WATER GLAZE	
	9 ounces white chocolate
	2 tablespoons water
	2 tablespoons simple syrup (½ cup powdered sugar plus ½ cup water)
	1 egg white

Split cooled chiffon layers in half. Use the three best ones for this cake.

Brush cut side of layers with rum.

*White
Chocolate
Rum Mousse*

Dissolve sugar in rum over low heat. Set aside.

Melt 4 ounces white chocolate in double boiler over hot water.

Add cream and stir well. Add the rum-sugar syrup to this and stir until smooth. Cool.

When really cool (not refrigerated), fold in 2 egg whites beaten to stiff peaks.

Fold in whipped cream carefully.

Chill in refrigerator for 30 minutes.

Spread this mousse thickly (use about ¾ cup) between each layer, and then thinly all over the sides and top of cake. Place in the freezer for 1 hour.

*White
Chocolate
Water Glaze*

Melt white chocolate and 2 tablespoons water over hot water, stirring very well until smooth.

Boil together ½ cup powdered sugar and ½ cup water for 10 minutes to make simple syrup.

Add 2 tablespoons syrup to melted white chocolate. Let it cool a bit.

Lightly beat egg white with a fork just to loosen it up.

Stir egg white into warm glaze mixture, blending well.

To Finish

When glaze is just warm (definitely not hot), pour it over the freezer-chilled mousse-covered cake. Use a spatula to smooth the sides, but try to pour the top evenly without any streaks or swirls. Press sliced almonds on the sides of the cake for a delicate finish.

Variation

If you would like to freeze this cake—and it is delicious when served semifrozen—substitute 3 cups of heavy cream, whipped with ¾ cup powdered sugar and flavored with 1 tablespoon rum, for the cooked egg mousse.

Coconut Cake

Sweet and coconutty, this classic layer cake is made with Yellow Chiffon Layers frosted with coconut butter cream and lavishly sprinkled with grated coconut. We have used both a fine shred of unsweetened coconut, toasted or plain, as well as a wide flake to finish this cake. Since supermarkets do not carry the same kind of coconut available commercially, you will have to choose between the unsweetened shreds found in health food stores and the canned sweetened variety.

1 recipe Yellow Chiffon Layers (page 126), baked and cooled

BASIC BUTTER CREAM FROSTING

6 tablespoons soft sweet butter
1 pound powdered sugar, sifted
1 egg, well beaten
¼ cup (approx.) light cream
1 teaspoon vanilla extract
1 teaspoon coconut or almond extract
8 ounces shredded coconut, sweetened or unsweetened

Prepare frosting by creaming together ingredients in the order given. Add the cream by tablespoonfuls until frosting is of spreading consistency. A big wooden spoon does fine, but so does an electric mixer. Beat until smooth and creamy. Add coconut extract.

This is best made as a two-layer cake. Place the first layer on a plate. Spread about ½ cup frosting. Cover with second layer.

Cover sides and top with remaining frosting. Generously sprinkle with shredded coconut. Enjoy.

An Easter Variation

For Easter we bake this cake in an egg-shaped mold, sprinkle with coconut, and then tie it up with a pastel butter cream ribbon. Lacking a special mold, the creative can cut out egg shapes from the baked layers. The wide bow is made with butter cream (colored if you wish) pressed with a pastry bag through a broad, flat tip. On a regular layer cake, those who enjoy nostalgic returns to childhood can decorate with jelly beans. The coconut can be tossed with a few drops of green food coloring so that you can hide the jelly beans in pale green grass.

Piña Colada Cake

This cake is a variation of our Coconut Cake with a piña colada filling that nicely complements the butter cream frosting.

1 recipe Yellow Chiffon Layers (page 126), baked and cooled

PIÑA COLADA WASH

2 ounces unsweetened pineapple juice from crushed pineapple (see below)
1 ounce white rum
2 ounces Coconut Creme (sold for mixing drinks)

1 recipe Basic Butter Cream Frosting (page 129)
4 tablespoons crushed pineapple, drained (Save juice.)
1 tablespoon dark rum
2 slices dried candied pineapple
4 ounces shredded coconut

Combine ingredients for Piña Colada Wash and brush both cake layers with it.

Mix together ½ cup frosting with 4 tablespoons crushed pineapple. Use this between the layers as a filling.

Stir 1 tablespoon rum into the rest of the frosting.

Frost the sides and top as noted for Coconut Cake.

Cut the dried pineapple into eight small wedges, then cut each of these into three slivers. Arrange them, fanning them out, around the top of the cake, marking each piece.

Sprinkle the sides with shredded coconut.

Strawberry Whipped-Cream Cake

A seasonal specialty, this beautiful dessert cake, crowned with the largest, most perfect berries available, would be ideal for a midsummer night's celebration. It is made with yellow chiffon cake rounds layered with fresh whipped cream and sliced fresh strawberries, garnished with eight large berries nested in swirls of whipped cream, sprinkled with sliced toasted almonds.

1 recipe Yellow Chiffon Layers (page 126), baked and cooled
1 pint fresh ripe strawberries
½ cup powdered sugar
3 cups heavy cream
1 teaspoon vanilla extract
2 ounces sliced toasted almonds

Carefully split cooled cake layers in half, placing on waxed paper until needed. If one layer should break, not to worry, a three-layer cake works very well!

Wash and dry strawberries. Reserve the eight best for the top. Slice the rest in about four slices each, divide into three equal portions.

Sift powdered sugar into cream. Add vanilla and whip until very thick.

Place first cake layer cut side down on cake plate. Spread with ¾ cup whipped cream.

Arrange one portion of sliced strawberries on top of the whipped cream, distributing evenly.

Repeat with the two remaining layers, always placing the cake with the cut side down, each time using about ¾ cup whipped cream and one portion of the sliced berries.

Cover the sides and top with the remaining whipped cream, smoothing with a knife or spatula. In the bakery we "comb" the sides with a decorator's tool that gives an attractive striped textured finish. It may be available in a local cookware shop.

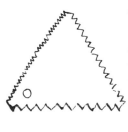

Press out eight swirls of cream using a pastry bag with a medium star tip and the reserved ½ cup of whipped cream. If you don't have this equipment, place eight tablespoon-size dollops of cream evenly on top of the cake, about 1 inch from the outside edge. To be sure they are lined up fairly straight, hold a ruler over the cake and make a small mark, top and bottom, where you will want to place the swirl.

Place one whole ripe berry in each of the swirls (or dollops), pointed end up.

Sprinkle some sliced toasted almonds lightly on the swirls surrounding each berry and also at the bottom edge of the cake, extending about 1–2 inches up from the plate.

Keep refrigerated until ready to serve. What could be better than strawberries and cream!

CHOCOLATE CHIFFON LAYERS

Yield: 1 8-inch layer cake

6 egg whites
1½ cups sugar
¾ cup vegetable oil
4 egg yolks
½ cup water
1 teaspoon vanilla
¾ cup unsweetened cocoa
1 cup flour
2 teaspoons baking powder
1 teaspoon baking soda
dash salt

Preheat oven to 350° F.

Butter two round 8-inch cake pans.

You will need three bowls (two large, one small).

Beat egg whites until soft peaks form. Gradually add ½ cup of the sugar and continue beating in large bowl of mixer until very stiff.

Mix oil, egg yolks, water, and vanilla in small bowl.

Sift dry ingredients together into the other large bowl: cocoa, flour, rest of sugar, baking powder and soda, and salt.

Add yolk mixture to dry mixture.

Fold in stiffly beaten egg whites and gently incorporate.

Pour into two prepared pans.

Bake at 350° for about 25 minutes, until sides shrink and top springs back when lightly pressed.

Chocolate Mousse Cake

The favorite of staff and customers alike, this cake is made with chocolate chiffon rounds layered with rich chocolate mousse, thinly covered overall with a bittersweet chocolate glaze, and finished with chocolate shavings on the sides. We make it in both two- and three-layer versions, but in our cookbook trials we found that four layers also worked well, although the cake gets a little harder to handle as it gets so tall. If by accident you damage a cake layer in splitting, just continue with a three-layer version; it is guaranteed to be both beautiful and absolutely satisfying to any chocoholics within reach! This cake freezes well and tastes like an ice-cream cake when the mousse is still semifrozen. In the summertime, many of our customers prefer to serve it that way. Rather than the more traditional egg mousse, we selected the whipped-cream version for the lighter touch it offers and its great ice-cream taste in the semifrozen state. In the section entitled "Many Mousses" we give several alternative mousse fillings. All of our many mousses can be substituted in this cake, using the procedures outlined below.

1 recipe Chocolate Chiffon Layers (page 133), baked and cooled

CHOCOLATE MOUSSE	*3 cups heavy whipping cream* *²⁄₃ cup unsweetened cocoa* *¾ cup sugar*
CHOCOLATE WATER GLAZE	*8 ounces semisweet chocolate* *½ cup water* *⅛ cup simple syrup (see directions below)* *⅛ cup beaten egg (½ egg)* *4-ounce semisweet chocolate bar, slightly softened in a warm place*

Carefully split cooled cake layers in half. Place carefully on waxed paper on a flat surface.

Mocha Kahlúa Cake

Clockwise from lower left: Black Forest Cake, The Grand Duchess, Strawberry Whipped Cream Cake

Mousse

Whip cream with sifted cocoa and sugar until quite firm, using an electric mixer.

Place first cake layer cut side down on cake plate. This prevents cake crumbs from coming loose in the mousse. Spread evenly with about ¾ cup mousse.

Repeat with additional layers, always placing cut side down.

Frost the entire cake, top and sides, with remaining mousse, covering thinly but completely. Chill in freezer about 1 hour.

Chocolate Water Glaze

Melt semisweet chocolate and water in heavy saucepan over low heat. Stir well to make a smooth chocolate syrup.

Blend in the ⅛ cup simple syrup, made by boiling ½ cup water and ½ cup powdered sugar together for 10 minutes.

Remove from heat and allow to cool for 3–4 minutes.

Blend in the beaten ½ egg and mix thoroughly.

Let glaze cool until it is just a little warmer than body temperature.

To Finish

Carefully shave warmed chocolate bar with a potato peeler or sharp paring knife. Use the entire 4-ounce bar.

Pour the warm glaze on the chilled mousse-covered cake, sides first, smoothing with a knife, followed by the top. The top should be as smooth and even as possible and should be poured on, not spread like a frosting.

Press the chocolate shavings all around the sides, working quickly before the glaze sets. Keep refrigerated until you are ready to indulge.

Variations

Recipes for these and other mousse fillings are in the next section.

1. Raspberry Mousse Cake is wonderful with chocolate layers brushed with raspberry liqueur. After you pour a chocolate glaze over the whole cake, pipe on the top of the cake concentric circles of red butter cream. Run a hot knife radiating out from the center through the circles to create a flower effect. Alternatively, arrange fresh (or drained frozen) raspberries artistically on the chocolate before it solidifies.

2. Orange Mousse Cake has chocolate layers brushed with orange liqueur. Garnish the top with glazed mandarin oranges or candied orange slices. You could also add the grated rind of one orange to the batter for the chocolate layers.

Many Mousses

Greyston Bakery offers a potpourri of mousses served in bittersweet chocolate cups, garnished with shaved chocolate. They include orange, raspberry, strawberry, cappuccino, and chocolate. These many mousses can also be used as cake fillings, following the directions for the Chocolate Mousse Cake in finishing. When using these mousses for cakes, a larger recipe is needed, as noted below.

Yield: 6 servings

6 semisweet chocolate dessert shells
4-ounce semisweet chocolate candy bar, slightly softened
¼ cup sliced almonds for garnish (optional)

BASIC MOUSSE
FROM FRUIT
PRESERVES

6 tablespoons preserves: orange, raspberry, or strawberry
2 cups heavy cream
⅛ cup powdered sugar

CHOCOLATE
MOUSSE

½ cup unsweetened cocoa sifted with ½ cup sugar
2 cups heavy cream

CAPPUCCINO
MOUSSE

2 tablespoons instant coffee dissolved in 1 tablespoon hot
*   water, then chilled*
2 cups heavy cream
½ cup powdered sugar

FRESH FRUIT
MOUSSE

1 cup crushed fresh fruit (strawberries, blueberries, cherries,
*   peaches) or drained defrosted frozen fruit. Reserve 6*
*   berries, cherries, or lemon-juice-dipped peach slices for*
*   decorating.*
2 cups heavy cream
½ cup powdered sugar

Basic Mousse from Fruit Preserves

Shave the semisweet chocolate with a potato peeler and set aside.

Mash up the measured fruit preserves with about ¼ cup heavy cream until soft and mushy.

Whip remaining cream and powdered sugar with electric mixer, pouring in the preserves mixture as it whips. Take care not to overbeat—butter is not the aim!

Using a pastry bag with a medium star tip, press mousse attractively into chocolate dessert shells. Alternatively, scoop into shells with an ice-cream scoop or mound with a spoon.

Sprinkle each shell with chocolate shavings or sliced almonds. Serve chilled.

Chocolate Mousse

Shave semisweet chocolate with a potato peeler and set aside.

Sift cocoa and sugar together. Whip cream with electric mixer, pouring in the cocoa mixture as it whips. Do not overbeat.

Fill dessert shells as directed above in Basic Mousse instructions.

Sprinkle each shell with chocolate shavings or sliced almonds. Serve chilled.

Cappuccino Mousse

Shave semisweet chocolate with a potato peeler and set aside.

Dissolve instant coffee in hot water and chill briefly in freezer.

Whip cream and powdered sugar with electric mixer, pouring in the coffee mixture as it whips. Take care not to overbeat.

Fill dessert shells as directed above in Basic Mousse instructions.

Sprinkle each shell with chocolate shavings or sliced almonds. Serve chilled.

Fresh Fruit Mousse

Shave semisweet chocolate with a potato peeler and set aside.

Crush fresh or frozen fruit with a fork.

Whip cream and powdered sugar with electric mixer. Take care not to overbeat. Add crushed fruit after cream is whipped.

Fill dessert shells as directed above in Basic Mousse instructions.

Sprinkle each shell with chocolate shavings or sliced almonds. Crown with reserved fruit. Serve chilled.

Mousses for Cake Fillings

Prepare mousse according to the directions given above, using one of the larger recipes that follow.

FRUIT MOUSSE
FILLING

3 cups heavy cream
¼ cup powdered sugar
8 tablespoons fruit preserves or 1½ cups diced fresh fruit

COFFEE MOUSSE
FILLING

3 cups heavy cream
¾ cup sifted powdered sugar
3 tablespoons coffee dissolved in 2 tablespoons hot water, then chilled

Black Forest Cake

In this, one of our most beautifully finished dessert cakes, the Chocolate Chiffon Layers are brushed with kirsch, lavishly layered with whipped cream and dark sweet cherries, and topped with bittersweet chocolate shavings and eight thin chocolate diamonds set into swirls of whipped cream to mark each piece. We tried to use the cherries on top, but the cherry juice seemed inevitably to run into the whipped cream, which just wasn't good for our commercial operation. At home, if you can serve this soon after assembling it, you can top the cake with well-drained cherries if you like. What we invented as an alternative, the thin chocolate diamonds, turn out to be both easy to make and most dramatically beautiful. We encourage you to give them a try.

1 recipe Chocolate Chiffon Layers (page 133), baked and
  cooled
2 cans dark sweet pitted cherries
4 ounces semisweet baking chocolate
½ cup powdered sugar
3 cups heavy cream
1 teaspoon vanilla
¼ cup kirsch or other brandy

Carefully split cooled cake layers in half, placing on waxed paper until needed. If one layer should break, the cake can be made with three layers.

Drain cherries, reserving ¼ cup juice. (In the summer you can use 2 cups fresh halved and pitted cherries soaked in a little extra kirsch and then well drained.)

Reserving 8 whole cherries, if desired for top, cut remaining cherries in half and divide into three portions. Place on folded paper towel to drain.

Melt 3 ounces chocolate over hot water in double boiler.

Set 1 ounce chocolate near stove to warm up.

For Diamond Decoration: Spread melted chocolate wafer-thin on the waxed paper, smoothing evenly with a knife. This will cover an area about 8–10 inches across. Place in refrigerator to harden. When very firm, cut into 8 diamonds about 1 x 1½ inches across. Peel off paper with spatula and chill until needed.

Sift powdered sugar into cream, add vanilla, and whip until very thick.

Mix together ½ cup kirsch or other brandy and ¼ cup cherry juice.

Place first layer cut side down on cake plate to prevent loose crumbs from coming up into the cream. Brush with kirsch mixture.

Reserve ½ cup whipped cream for swirls.

Spread about ¾ cup whipped cream on layer, then arrange one portion of the halved cherries on the cream. Repeat with remaining layers.

Place the top layer on. Do not brush it with cherry-brandy juice; this prevents the cherry juice from "bleeding" into the cream. Spread whipped cream on top, about ½ inch thick. Cover sides and smooth with a knife. Refrigerate.

With sharp knife or potato peeler, shave reserved warmed chunk of chocolate into little bits (this can be "chocolate dust" and not actual shavings).

With a medium star tip, press the reserved whipped cream through a pastry bag, forming 8 swirls evenly placed about 1 inch in from outside edge of cake. You can substitute dollops of cream if you lack the proper equipment. The swirls can be positioned with the help of a ruler held over the cake, making small marks, top and bottom, where you will place the swirls.

Either place one large whole pitted cherry, very well drained, on each swirl, or place the chocolate diamonds on edge in the swirls with the 1-inch side going up. This gives an airy, wing-like decoration that is quite dazzling.

Sprinkle chocolate shavings lightly around each swirl and around the base of cake, coming up about 1 inch on the sides. Refrigerate until ready to serve.

Mocha Kahlúa Cake

Melding together the flavors of coffee and chocolate, the dark chiffon layers are brushed with Kahlúa liqueur, then frosted with coffee butter cream and decorated with chocolate "coffee beans." This makes an excellent adult birthday cake and is delicious with a cup of good aromatic coffee for dessert.

1 recipe Chocolate Chiffon Layers (page 133), baked and cooled

COFFEE BUTTER
CREAM
FROSTING

6 tablespoons sweet butter
1 pound sifted powdered sugar
1 egg, well beaten
¼ cup (approx.) light cream
1 teaspoon vanilla
1 tablespoon Maxwell House instant coffee dissolved in
  1 tablespoon boiling water (Do not use freeze-dried coffee.
  This brand works best; others produce an off color after
  2–3 days in the refrigerator.)
¼ cup Kahlúa liqueur
8 chocolate "coffee bean" candies (available in gourmet
  groceries or confectionaries)

Prepare frosting by creaming together ingredients in the order given. Add cream by tablespoonfuls until frosting is of spreading consistency. A big wooden spoon works fine, but so does an electric mixer. Beat until very smooth and creamy.

This works best as a conventional two-layer cake. Place first layer on plate, brush with Kahlúa, and then spread about ½ cup frosting. Repeat with remaining layer.

Reserve ½ cup frosting for decoration.

Frost sides and top with remaining frosting, swirling the sides attractively, or "comb" the sides with the special decorator's tool (see page 131).

Using a ruler held over the cake, mark eight equidistant points around the top of the cake, about 1 inch in from the edge.

Using a pastry bag with a medium star tip, press out a ribbon of frosting around the top outer edge of the cake, looping the ribbon at the eight marked places.

Place a candy coffee bean on each of the loops in the ribbon.

Alternatively, press out eight swirls or use spoonfuls of frosting to form a nest for the candy coffee beans. Shaved bittersweet chocolate could substitute for the coffee beans.

Variation   This cake is delicious when layered with cappuccino mousse and then frosted with butter cream. See page 137 for mousse recipe.

Chocolate Mint Cake

Using the same basic recipe and procedures given for the Mocha Kahlúa Cake (page 140), substitute 1 teaspoon mint extract (or more to taste) for the vanilla in the frosting, and eliminate the coffee. Alternatively, add 1–2 tablespoons crème de menthe to the frosting rather than the extract. Then brush the layers with crème de menthe liqueur. For decorating, use either sprigs of fresh mint in the summertime or after-dinner mint wafers set on edge in the dollops of butter cream—with very delicious results.

Variation   One inventive tester, after failing to find mint extract at the market, melted down six after-dinner mints (the large, thin square ones) and added them to the frosting, giving a pale chocolate hue and a definite minty flavor. She sprinkled some shaved semisweet chocolate on the top, and it looked lovely!

Happy Birthday Chocolate Cake

Chocolate with chocolate—our dark chiffon layers are filled and frosted with chocolate butter cream. This is the perfect birthday cake and seems to shout for a glass of cold milk for an after-school snack. To decorate, use a fine tip on a pastry bag and write your message in vanilla butter cream colored with a few drops of food coloring if you wish.

1 recipe Chocolate Chiffon Layers (page 133), baked and
cooled

CHOCOLATE
BUTTER CREAM

6 tablespoons soft butter
1 pound powdered sugar
1 egg, well beaten
¼ cup light cream
1 teaspoon vanilla
2 ounces unsweetened baker's chocolate, melted
3 ounces semisweet chocolate for shavings (optional)

Using an electric mixer, cream the butter, sugar, egg, cream, and vanilla. Whip until very smooth. Reserve ½ cup vanilla frosting for writing "Happy Birthday" if desired. Add melted chocolate and mix very well. Reserve ½ cup chocolate frosting for finishing swirls.

Fill and frost, making a two-layer cake.

With a pastry bag and a small round tip, write your message with the vanilla butter cream. Then, using a medium star tip, press the reserved chocolate frosting into a ribbon all around the top edge of cake.

We "comb" the sides with our special decorator's tool. You can swirl the sides attractively or just leave smooth. Chocolate shavings from semisweet chocolate could also be pressed on the sides. The best way to make shavings is to warm up the chocolate near the stove and then use a sharp knife or potato peeler to shave off slivers.

INDEX